Psalm 29 through Time and Tradition

Princeton Theological Monograph Series

K. C. Hanson, Charles M. Collier, and D. Christopher Spinks,
Series Editors

Recent volumes in the series:

Richard Valantasis et al., editors
The Subjective Eye: Essays in Honor of Margaret Miles

Anette Ejsing
A Theology of Anticipation: A Constructive Study of C. S. Peirce

Caryn Riswold
Coram Deo: Human Life in the Vision of God

Paul O. Ingram, editor
Constructing a Relational Cosmology

Michael G. Cartwright
Practices, Politics, and Performance: Toward a Communal Hermeneutic for Christian Ethics

David A. Ackerman
Lo, I Tell You a Mystery: Cross, Resurrection, and Paraenesis in the Rhetoric of 1 Corinthians

Lloyd Kim
Polemic in the Book of Hebrews: Anti-Judaism, Anti-Semitism, Supersessionism?

Psalm 29 through Time and Tradition

Edited by
LOWELL K. HANDY

◆PICKWICK *Publications* • Eugene, Oregon

PSALM 29 THROUGH TIME AND TRADITION
Princeton Theological Monograph Series 110

Copyright © 2009 Wipf and Stock. All rights reserved. Except for brief quotations in critical articles or reviews, no part of this book may be reproduced in any manner without prior written permission from the publisher. Write: Permissions, Wipf and Stock Publishers, 199 W. 8th Ave., Suite 3, Eugene, OR 97401.

Pickwick Publications
A Division of Wipf and Stock Publishers
199 W. 8th Ave., Suite 3
Eugene, OR 97401

www.wipfandstock.com

ISBN 13: 978-1-55635-529-5

Cataloging-in-Publication data:

Psalm 29 through time and tradition / Edited by Lowell K. Handy.

    Eugene, Ore.: Pickwick Publications, 2008

    Princeton Theological Monograph Series 110

    xii + 148 p. ; 23 cm.

    Includes bibliographies and index

    ISBN 13: 978-1-55635-529-5

    1. Bible. O.T. Psalms—Criticism, interpretation, etc. 2. Bible. O.T. Psalms 29—Criticism, interpretation, etc. I. Handy, Lowell K., 1949–. II. Title. III. Series.

Manufactured in the U.S.A.

Contents

Acknowledgements / vii

Abbreviations / ix

List of Contributors / xi

1. Introduction—Lowell K. Handy / 1
2. Adapting Psalm 29 through Translation—Brooks Schramm / 9
3. Echoes of "the Voice": Psalm 29 in the Fathers—Jeffrey B. Gibson / 25
4. Psalm 29 in Jewish Psalms Commentary (*Midrash Tehillim*): King David's Instructions for Synagogue Prayer—Esther Menn and David Sandmel / 37
5. The Psalms and Psalm 29 among Syrian Christians—Paul S. Russell / 52
6. Not Elijah's God: Medieval Jewish and Christian Interpretation of Psalm 29—Stacy Davis / 69
7. Luther and Calvin Read Psalm 29—Lowell K. Handy / 79
8. The Liturgical Use of Psalm 29—Bert Polman / 90
9. Singing Psalm 29 Faithfully—Emily R. Brink / 99

10   Gods of Glory Ought to Thunder: The Canaanite Matrix of Psalm 29—*Dennis Pardee* and *Nancy Pardee* / 115

11   Psalm 29 in African Indigenous Churches in Nigeria— *David Tuesday Adamo* / 126

Index of Proper Names / 145

Acknowledgements

Deep thanks is extended to the following for use of copyrighted material:

Scripture quotations, unless otherwise credited, are from the New Revised Standard Version of the Bible, copyright © 1989 by the Division of Christian Education of the National Council of Churches in the U.S.A., and used by permission.

Jewish Publication Society for Psalm 29 from the Tanakh: The Holy Scriptures: The New JPS Translation according to the Traditional Hebrew Text, Philadelphia: JPS, 1985.

Sing Glory. Tune by Michael Perry, music by Norman Warren. © 1973 The Jubilate Group, administered by Hope Publishing Company, Carol Stream, IL, 60188.

And to the following individuals for allowing quotations from their work: Margaret M. Mitchell and Stephen D. Ryan.

Abbreviations

AB	Anchor Bible
ABD	*Anchor Bible Dictionary*
ACCSOT	Ancient Christian Commentary on Scripture. Old Testament
AIC	African Indigenous Churches
ALASP	Abhandlungen zur Literatur Alt-Syren-Palästinas und Mesopotamiens
ArBib	The Aramaic Bible
b.	Babylonian Talmud (*Babli*)
Bib	*Biblica*
BibSem	Biblical Seminar
BlTh	*Black Theology*
BTT	Bibel des tous les temps
CH	*Church History*
Comm	*Communia*
COS	*The Context of Scripture*
CSCO	Corpus scriptorum christianorum orientalium
EncJud	*Encyclopaedia Judaica*
FC	Fathers of the Church
FIOTL	Formation and Interpretation of Old Testament Literature
HO	Handbuch der Orientalistik
HTR	*Harvard Theological Review*
HvTSt	*Hervormde teologiese studies*
JECS	*Journal of Early Christian Studies*
JJS	*Journal of Jewish Studies*
JR	*Journal of Religion*

JSOTSup	*Journal for the Study of the Old Testament Supplement Series*
LEC	Library of Early Christianity
LQ	*Lutheran Quarterly*
NRSV	New Revised Standard Version
OrChrAn	*Orientalia christiana analecta*
RB	*Revue biblique*
RefLitM	*Reformed Liturgy and Music*
SacEr	*Sacris Erudiri*
SBLSymS	Society of Biblical Literature Symposium Series
SFSHJ	South Florida Studies in the History of Judaism
SJOT	*Scandinavian Journal of the Old Testament*
SJT	*Scottish Journal of Theology*
VTSup	Supplements to Vetus Testamentum
WBC	Word Biblical Commentary
WGRW	Writings from the Greco-Roman World
WSA	The Works of Saint Augustine
y.	Jerusalem Talmud (Yerushalmi)
YJS	Yale Judaica Series

Contributors

David Tuesday Adamo (Ph.D., Baylor University). Professor and Dean of Faculty of Arts and Humanities, Kogi State University.

Emily Brink (Ph.D., Northwestern University). Senior Research Fellow, Calvin Institute of Christian Worship, Calvin College.

Stacy Davis (Ph.D., University of Notre Dame). Assistant Professor, Saint Mary's College, Notre Dame, Indiana.

Jeffrey Gibson (Ph.D., University of Oxford). Lecturer in Humanities and Religious Studies, Harry S Truman College and Columbia College, Chicago.

Lowell K. Handy (Ph.D., University of Chicago). Indexer/Analyst, American Theological Library Association.

Esther Menn (Ph.D., University of Chicago). Professor of Old Testament, Lutheran School of Theology at Chicago.

Dennis Pardee (Ph.D., University of Chicago). Professor, Oriental Institute of the University of Chicago.

Nancy Pardee (Ph.D., University of Chicago). Adjunct Instructor, Saint Xavier University.

Bert Polman (Ph.D., University of Minnesota). Professor and Chair of Music, and Senior Research Fellow, Calvin Institute of Christian Worship, Calvin College.

Paul S. Russell (Ph.D., The Catholic University of America). Academic Dean, St. Joseph of Arimathea Anglican Theological College.

David Fox Sandmel (Ph.D., University of Pennsylvania). Crown Ryan Professor of Jewish Studies, Catholic Theological Union.

Brooks Schramm (Ph.D., University of Chicago). Associate Professor of Biblical Studies. Lutheran Theological Seminary, Gettysburg.

1

Introduction

Lowell K. Handy

PSALM 29 IS A HEBREW POEM. BEYOND THAT FLAT COMMENT IT CAN be stated that this poem forms a part of the biblical book of Psalms and thereby becomes more than simply an ancient verse. Judaism and Christianity have accepted this poetic creation as part of their sacred text engendering a myriad of interpretations for the meaning of the short piece. Unlike many other biblical passages, Psalm 29 has a secure textual form. That is, the Hebrew of the poem is almost universally agreed to have been transmitted with little or no changes. Variant spellings of the Hebrew words notwithstanding, the words that form the psalm are certain.

What is not certain is the meaning of the words themselves at the time of the poem's composition. Indeed, the time of composition of the poem remains a debated question among biblical scholars with a range of roughly a thousand years marked by the twelfth century BCE as the earliest seriously suggested date to the third century BCE as the latest. Most attempts to date the poem range more narrowly from the tenth to the seventh centuries BCE, but no one knows when or by whom the text was written. On the other hand, it is generally agreed that the poem had its origin in the religious circles of the Jerusalem temple.

Since the poem's incorporation into the book of Psalms, the meaning of the work has been analyzed by every branch of Judaism and Christianity. This volume of essays seeks to demonstrate for the interested reader how such an uncomplicated biblical text has been read through time and by different traditions in an effort to illustrate the diversity with which the Bible as a whole has been treated. It is imperative that anyone reading the Bible understand that no matter what tradition they themselves inhabit, from devout Orthodox Judaism to radical secular materialism, however they read the text, it is neither how everyone else reads, nor others have understood, the same words. Indeed, the majority of people look at the same words on the page and do not see what any given reader sees. This diversity can be confusing, but ought to be understood by anyone reading biblical texts for any purpose from idle curiosity to doctrinal meditation.

This confusion may be seen beginning simply with the numbering of the psalm. For this volume the psalm is numbered 29 with the Jewish (adopted by Protestants) numbering system. While most, but not all, Christian Bibles have the same basic Psalms text divided into 150 psalms, in traditions based on the Greek Septuagint Psalter some psalms have been combined into a single psalm and others divided into two psalms thereby changing the numbers assigned particular psalms. Thus, in the Vulgate (the traditional Latin Bible of the Roman Catholic Church) and in many Eastern Orthodox Churches this psalm is numbered 28. Fortunately, the verse numbers within Psalm 29 are not among those in the book of Psalms that differ radically between the Jewish and Christian Bibles. Save for the heading to the psalm (*mizmor ldawid* = psalm of/for David), which is included in verse one of the Hebrew text, but unnumbered in Protestant texts, the verse numbers correspond to the same poetic lines.

In most traditions that have used the book of Psalms as a sacred text Psalm 29 is a liturgical text. The psalm remains a part of the liturgy in both Jewish and Christian worship. The earliest record of Psalm 29 in a worship setting comes from the Talmud (*b. Rosh HaShanah* 30b; *Sukkah* 55a) where it is reported that Psalm 29 was the ritual recitation for sacrifices in the temple on Rosh Hashanah (New Years) and The Feast of Booths (Tabernacles). Of course, in these services Psalm 29 was recited from memory and in Hebrew. Moreover, the rabbis deemed speaking the sections of the psalm concerning water (verses 3–5, 7–9) sufficient remembrance of God to allow the safe drinking of water on the Sabbath (*Pesaḥim* 112a). The final line of the psalm was understood to promise that students of Jewish wisdom would bring peace to the world (*b. Berakhoth* 64a) and that there would be peace in the world to come (*Uqtzin*).

Leaping ahead a millennium, the psalms were widely known in the European Christian Middle Ages as wisdom literature, read in their entirety as religious texts and for meditation. Psalm 29, like all of the psalms, was known among the devout in adapted literary formations composed for religious reflection. For those who wanted the meaning of their Scripture more transparent as well as more readable, there were Latin rhyming poems for the literate devotional set. These poems rewrote the psalms with an intent to display the basic themes to be meditated upon by the pious Christian and interestingly enough for Psalm 29 (the medieval European church's Ps 28) this meant mostly the opening and closing sections of the psalm. From the thirteenth-century the following shortened form of Psalm 29 concentrated on praising God, in the person of Jesus, as king:

> Afferte arietum filios afferte,
> Et offerte domino laudis uota certe
> Vox uirtutis domini personat exerte.
> Sedebit rex dominus iudicans aperte
> Sed tu, Ihesu domine, ut saluemur per te,
> Nostris a nequiciis faciem auerte. (Colker, 345)

The emphasis on honoring God and the resulting peace on earth, to the exclusion of the glorious storm imagery of the original Hebrew, also distinguishes this fifteenth-century rendition:

> Trinum deum adorate,
> Vora laudis ymmolate
> Vere, dei filii!
> Cuius rex in septem donis
> Corda replet cunctis bonis:
> Nostri spes exilii.
>
> Huic laudem et honorem
> Omnes iusti per amorem
> Dicant in ecclesia
> In eternum qui regnabit,
> Cum uirtute ministrabit
> Pacem in victoria. (Orbán, 426)

It is important to remember that Psalm 29 for a large portion of the Protestant population of Europe and North America was not in Hebrew, nor was it in Latin and it was not read from the book of Psalms, but was known from the Psalter as sung. And for many, particularly in Reformed traditions, the text of Psalm 29 simply *was* that of the Geneva Psalter. The 1560 English lyric incorporated both traditional Christian and contemporary Calvinist translation elements:

> Giue vnto the Lord, ye sonnes of the mightie; giue vnto the Lord glorie and strength. Giue vnto the Lord glorie *due* unto his Name: worship the Lord in the glorious Sanctuarie. The voice of the Lord *is* vpon the waters: the God of glorie maketh it to thunder: the Lord *is* vpon the great waters. The voice of the Lord *is* mightie: the voice of the Lord *is* glorious. The voice of the Lord breaketh the cedres: yea, the Lord breaketh the cedres of Lebanón. He maketh them also to leape like a calfe: Lebanón *also* and Shirión like a yong vnicorne. The voice of the Lord deuideth the flames of fyre. The voice of the Lord maketh the wilderness to tremble: the Lord maketh the wilderness of Kadésh to tremble. The voice of the Lord maketh the hindes to calue & discouereth the forests: *Therefore* in his Temple doeth euerie man speake of *his* glorie. The Lord sitteth vpon the flood, and the Lord doeth remaine King for euer. The Lord shal giue strength vnto his people: ye Lord shal blesse his people with peace. (*Geneva Psalter*)

Some interpretations of the psalm will no doubt strike any modern reader as just incomprehensible. Having verse six explained as a reference to monotheism can only make sense if one realizes that this interpretation by Theodoret of Cyrus was based on the Septuagint Greek translation which included a "unicorn." Then one would need to understand that for many in the early church the entire psalm was a commission for Christian baptism. Finally, the symbolic reading of Old Testament poetry by Christian pastoral clergy for use in congregational life produces imaginative and creative meanings. So, for Theodoret, the single horn of the unicorn represents the monotheism now a part of the Christian convert being baptized. Finding the seven Catholic sacraments in the psalm can only strike non-Catholic readers (and no doubt many Catholic readers as well) as absurd, but Robert Bellarmin (1542–1621) found Psalm 29 a fine scriptural authority against Protestant reformers who were reducing the sacraments to only two. Again, for many Protestants the reading of the seven voices in the poem as the seven gifts of the Holy Spirit, a tradition of the "Spiritual Reading" of the psalm, will be just as foreign; though for Pentecostals a reading that finds spiritual gifts here might well seem quite natural. On the other hand, for most Christian readers, the traditional reading of Revelation 10:2–4 as a reference to Psalm 29 should not cause surprise.

In academic circles it is not uncommon for biblical texts to be divorced from religious traditions more recent than the first century CE. The psalms have been and remain central to most Jewish and Christian faith communities, so chapters on Psalters and liturgy have been included. In adapting psalms for use in Christian choral settings it has not been unusual to find the text adapted accordingly. A long train of theological, exegetical, and compositional traditions combined to produce a lyric such as that by Charles Wesley (1707–1788):

> Ye worms, that wear an earthly crown,
>   Before the King of kings bow down,
> Glory to God and worship give:
>   Honour is due to God alone;
> Fountain of power your Maker own,
>   And happy in his service live.
>
> With joy the Lord of hosts proclaim,
> Extol the great Jehovah's name,
>   His praises let your lives declare;
> His image be your costly dress,
> Your beauty be his holiness,
>   His love your royal diadem wear.
>
> His voice upon the waters is,
> (What monarch hath a voice like his?)
>   Loud as ten thousand seas it roars;
> Above the firmament he sits,
> And earth to the Great King submits,
>   And heaven its sovereign Lord adores.
>
> The glorious God majestic speaks;
> From the dark cloud his terror breaks,
>   And waving sheets of lightning shine.
> The' impetuous hurricane of sound
> Rives the strong oaks, and shakes the ground:
>   For thunder is the Voice Divine.
>
> Jehovah's voice the cedar rends,
> And all the pride of Lebanon bends,
>   And strips and tears the scatter'd trees;

> The hinds affrighted calve and die,
> While mix'd with flames the thunders fly,
>> And rock the howling wilderness.
>
> Creation hears his voice, and quakes;
> Sea, earth, and hell, and heaven he shakes,
>> Firm on his everlasting throne!
> But all who in his temple praise,
> And love and thank him for his grace,
>> Shall never, never be cast down.
>
> High above all their Savior sits,
> And earth to the Great King submits,
>> And heaven its sovereign Lord adores;
> Jehovah sends his succours thence,
> Arms them with his omnipotence,
>> And all their strength divine restores.
>
> Jesus, to all who dare believe,
> The fulness of his power shall give;
>> The gospel hope, the glorious prize,
> The perfect love, the perfect peace,
> The everlasting righteousness,
>> The heaven-insuring Paradise.

It is hoped that reading the contributions collected here will allow one to reread Wesley's Psalm 29 and understand in a much better way how he understood the biblical text and what he was attempting to do with it.

As one of the "Nature Psalms" in many Orthodox Christian traditions, Psalm 29 has been recently enlisted in the eco-theology of the twenty-first century church. Here God is the lord of nature; humanity is called to recognize divine sovereignty over the earth and accept responsibility for caring for the world. In many Christian Orthodox traditions the experience of God's presence in the wildest regions of God's world has a long and honored history; Psalm 29 displays this connection through the vivid juxtaposition of the "Word of the Lord" and the frenzied behavior of the natural world. So, for example, a Russian Orthodox reading of Psalm 29 understands the work as reflecting the majesty of God in a thunderstorm (Lopukhin). The "sons of God" are understood to be the human rulers being invited to worship God in the temple. The "voice of the Lord" is thunder and the "fiery flame" of verse 7 is lightening. Verses 5–10 are all understood as events of a ferocious storm: cedars broken to kindling, winds blowing up sand and dust, animals trembling and giving birth prematurely in terror, a forest denuded of leaves, flood waters pouring from the clouds. Yet the Lord reigns as if on a throne over it all and, for those who pay homage to the divine majesty and power, there will be peace and protection from enemies.

While introductions to the history of the interpretation of Scripture have become common in the past couple decades, these works by necessity have been general surveys of movements and outstanding biblical exegetes. This volume hopes to provide a quite specific example of biblical interpretation in several religious traditions by exegetes both famous and little-known outside of their own tradition. A background in some of these traditions therefore becomes necessary to understand the place of psalms and of Psalm 29 in diverse cultures and short contextual surveys are provided for traditions less known in the western church. The following chapters will give a sampling of Jewish and Christian understandings and uses of Psalm 29. A concerted effort to deal with the text at a close level is intended to provide the reader with material to consider, with biblical text in hand, how others have understood this text through time and traditions.

The origin of this book itself has a history of a quarter century. In 1974 I finished my masters thesis at the University of Iowa on "The Origin and Conversion of Psalm 29." The department informed me that the final proposed chapter was not to be included as the work was too long already. I had hoped, as the final display of "converting" the psalm, to show how Jewish and Christian commentators had understood the psalm. I never gave up an interest in the topic, but realized through the years, that no one, certainly not I, had the competence to cover even a fraction of the material. So this work, still a mere wee fraction of a percent of the interpretations of Psalm 29, is in a sense that final chapter and I wish to thank the contributors for their work on this project. When I first wanted to write the history of interpretation of Psalm 29 such histories were not in fashion. Things have changed. This book arose from the Bible through Time and Tradition section of the 2004 Midwest Region of the Society of Biblical Literature. Four chapters are expansions of section papers by Stacy Davis, Jeffrey Gibson, Lowell Handy, and Esther Menn presented at that conference. As a final irony, the 2007 flood waters of Des Plaines, Illinois, engulfed my copy of my M.A. thesis, but not the manuscript pages for this book.

Bibliography

Alonso-Schökel, Luis. *Treinta Salmos: Poesia y Oración.* 2nd ed. Madrid: Cristianidad, 1986.

Colker, Marvin L. "A Christianized Latin Psalter in Rhythmic Verse." *SacEr* 30 (1987–1988) 329–408.

Holladay, William L. *The Psalms through Three Thousand Years: Prayerbook of a Cloud of Witnesses.* Minneapolis: Fortress, 1993.

Lopukhin, A. P. *Tolkovaia Bibliia: ili Kommentarii na vse knigi Sv. Pisaniia Vetkago i Novago Zaveta.* Repr. ed. [Translated for the editor by Nina Shultz.] Stockholm: Institute of Bible Translation, 1987.

Mathew, K. V. "Ecology and Faith in the Old Testament." In *Upon the Wings of Wider Ecumenism: Essays and Tributes in Honour of Rev. Dr. M. J. Joseph,* edited by P. Gandhi and K. John, 58–63. Delhi: ISPCK/ECC, 2006.

Mowinkel, Sigmund. *The Psalms in Israel's Worship.* Translated by D. R. Ap-Thomas. 1962. Reprinted with a Foreword by James L. Crenshaw, Grand Rapids: Eerdmans, 2004.

O'Keefe, John J. "'A Letter That Killeth': Toward a Reassessment of Antiochene Exegesis, or Diodore, Theodore, and Theodoret on the Psalms." *JECS* 8 (2000) 83–104.

Orbán, Arpad Peter. "Das *Psalteerium Rigmizatum* in einer Handschrift der Kirchenbibliothek von St. Marien in Danzig (Ms. Mar. Q 26)." *SacEr* 32 (1991) 395–502.

Thompson, John L. *Reading the Bible with the Dead: What You Can Learn from the History of Exegesis that You Can't Learn from Exegesis Alone.* Grand Rapids: Eerdmans, 2007.

Wesley, Charles. *A Poetical Version of Nearly the Whole of the Psalms of David by the Rev. Charles Wesley, M.A.* Edited by Henry Fish. 2nd ed. London: John Mason, 1854.

Wright, William Aldis, editor. *The Hexaplar Psalter: Being the Book of Psalms in Six English Versions.* Cambridge: Cambridge University Press, 1911.

2

Adapting Psalm 29 through Translation

Brooks Schramm

Translation as Primary Act of Interpretation

TRANSLATION OF A TEXT BECOMES NECESSARY WHENEVER THE LANGUAGE of that text has become a foreign language to its primary hearers and readers. Already in antiquity the Hebrew Bible was being rendered into different languages, first by Jews and then by Christians, in order to accommodate the various linguistic communities that the respective religions were reaching. Jews translated the Bible into Greek (the Septuagint) and Aramaic (the Targum). Christians translated the Bible into Latin (Old Latin, Vulgate), Ethiopic, Coptic, Syriac (the earliest portions of which may have originally been Jewish), and other languages.

In the translation of sacred texts like the Bible, the stakes are especially high because the new translated text tends to be regarded as sacred as well. This has clearly been the case in Christianity, although less so in Judaism. Once a new translation has been received by the community for which it is intended, it can replace the original. Where the Bible is concerned "the Bible in translation" can become "the Bible" for a particular linguistic community such that the original falls away for all practical purposes.

Ancient Bible translators were faced with the same dilemma that faces all translators, which is whether to translate more literally, more periphrastically (in a round-about manner), or somewhere in between. As a rule (and perhaps surprisingly) these translators of the Bible normally opted for the more literalistic form, sticking very closely to the wording of the original text and giving word-for-word equivalents whenever possible. This translational tendency has remained the case throughout the history of Bible translating with only rare exceptions (as with the ancient Targum or the modern *Living Bible*). This means that the interpretive moves made by these translators tend to be subtle ones and can easily go unnoticed. In addition, a seemingly simple translational change can often signal a significant shift in meaning, even to the point of making the translation say the exact opposite of what the original says.

Studying various translations of the Hebrew Bible (ancient, early-modern and modern) and comparing them closely with the original language is a fascinating exercise. Because translation is by definition an act of interpretation, indeed the most basic act of interpretation, when one studies the Bible in its ancient translations one is in fact studying our earliest commentaries on the Bible. The only way truly to appreciate this, however, is to place the translation right alongside of the original and then one can actually see the interpretive moves made by the translator.

The factor that perhaps trumps all others when it comes to the translation of the Bible is that of theology or the religious conviction of the translator. The Bible after all was not just any book for those who expended the immense amount of labor required in order to translate it. The translators were both deeply religious Jews and Christians as well as deeply invested in these texts as the written word of God. But what happens when a translator encounters a text in the Bible that seems to be in tension with, or even contradict, other texts in the Bible? Or, what happens when a translator encounters a text that seems to be in tension with, or even contradict, the religious convictions of the translator him/herself or of the community of which the translator is a part? This is where things can become interesting. Sometimes translators will leave the text as is, that is: they will allow the theological problem to remain (apparently relying on subsequent commentary to clarify the matter). At other times they will subtly alter the original text so as to take the edge off of the problem, or to make it less readily apparent to the reader or hearer. At still other times the translator will boldly change the text so as to eliminate the theological problem altogether.

Psalm 29 provides an excellent case-study for the dynamics discussed above. In its original Hebrew form the psalm begins with what clearly looks to be polytheistic imagery. But by the time the psalm was being translated into other languages all of the translators were themselves monotheists! In addition, the psalm portrays YHWH, the god of Israel, in ways that look very much like the Canaanite nature- or storm-god, Baal. So much so that if one were to substitute the name Baal for the name YHWH throughout Psalm 29 one would have a fine Canaanite psalm. How have translators, ancient (Greek, Aramaic, Latin), early-modern (Luther, King James), and modern (NRSV, NJPS) handled these and other problems in this psalm? It is to this question that we now turn.

Psalm 29 in Hebrew

First we look at the source of the problems: Psalm 29 in the language in which it was originally composed, Hebrew. A very literal, even wooden, translation of the Hebrew text of Psalm 29 looks like this:

> [1] A psalm of David
>
> Ascribe to YHWH, O sons of (the) G(g)od(s), ascribe to YHWH glory and strength.
>
> [2] Ascribe to YHWH the glory of his name, bow down to YHWH in holy splendor.
>
> [3] The voice of YHWH upon the waters, the God of glory thundered,
>
> YHWH upon mighty waters
>
> [4] The voice of YHWH in strength, the voice of YHWH in splendor
>
> [5] The voice of YHWH breaking cedars, and YHWH shattered the cedars of Lebanon.
>
> [6] He made Lebanon skip like a calf, and Sirion like a young wild ox.
>
> [7] The voice of YHWH hewing flames of fire.
>
> [8] The voice of YHWH will convulse the wilderness,
>
> YHWH will convulse the wilderness of Kadesh.
>
> [9] The voice of YHWH will bring hinds into labor, and stripped forests bare,
>
> and in his temple all (are) saying "Glory."
>
> [10] YHWH sat at the flood and YHWH sat as king forever.

> [11] YHWH will give strength to his people, YHWH will bless his people with peace.

The Hebrew version of the psalm presents immediate problems for anyone who would translate it. The first is that of the Hebrew verb. Biblical Hebrew has no linking verb ("to be"). In addition, the verb tenses in Hebrew (a Semitic language) do not match up well with Indo-European languages (like English). Hebrew verbs fall under the categories of completed action (Perfect tense), incompleted action (Imperfect tense), and something like continuous or ongoing action (Participle). The issue of how to render these verb tenses accurately into Indo-European languages is complicated in the extreme and continues to be debated by grammarians to this day. The issue is even more complicated when it comes to Hebrew poetry like the psalms. In poetry issues such as balance, rhythm, sound, accentuation, and other acoustic devices are often more important than sheer verbal tense and thus a Hebrew poet can use two or more tenses in the very same verse. The wooden (and in some places virtually nonsensical) translation presented above is designed both to highlight the awkwardness of rendering the Hebrew verbs of Psalm 29 into English in a strictly literal manner; it also alerts the reader to those places in the text where translators have to make explicit decisions regarding verbal tense or in regard to the insertion of a verb in order to make their translation make sense.

A second, easily overlooked problem occurs in Psalm 29:1 and relates to the personal name of the god of Israel, commonly referred to as the tetragrammaton (the four-letter name). The four letters (YHWH) represent the four consonants of the Hebrew name. At some point in the history of ancient Israel, and certainly by the time of the translation of the Hebrew Bible into Greek in the mid-third century BCE, Jews had ceased to pronounce this name as a sign of reverence. Instead, the Hebrew word *'adonay* ("lord") was pronounced in its place. As a result, over time the actual original pronunciation was lost. The well-known term, Jehovah, resulted from a misunderstanding of the Hebrew vowel-pointing system by certain Christian scholars during the sixteenth century; it found its way into the Geneva Bible of 1599 (six times) and into the King James Bible of 1611 (four times). In spite of its subsequent popularity, the term is meaningless. The current scholarly reconstruction is that the name was originally pronounced *Yahweh*. How the tetragrammaton is represented in translation is one of the more interesting theological issues in the history of the translation of the Bible.

A third problem also occurs already in Psalm 29:1 in the phrase rendered "sons of (the) G(g)od(s)." The exact Hebrew phrase in question occurs only one other time in the Bible (Psalm 89:6). The Hebrew term here rendered "G(g)od(s)" is ’elim, the plural form of ’El. In ancient Canaan ’El was the proper name of the grandfather deity of the Canaanite pantheon (and the father of Baal). In the Hebrew Bible this word is used as a generic word for "G/god." It can also be seen in proper names like Israel, Bethel, Daniel, Samuel, Gabriel, Michael, Raphael, and many others. The more common generic word for G/gods in the Bible is ’elohim, a word that is plural in form but which can have either a singular or plural meaning. So, for example: "You shall have no other gods [’elohim] before me" but "In the beginning when God [’elohim] created the heavens and the earth." Either context or grammatical agreement between subject and verb usually decide the issue in Hebrew. The difference between the two words is as follows: while the formally plural word ’elohim has both singular and plural meanings, the formally plural word ’elim always has a plural meaning, at least as it is used in the Bible. Technically speaking, then, "sons of ’elohim would be ambiguous, but "sons of ’elim," which is used in this psalm, is not. How will translators handle this seemingly clear polytheistic reference?

The reader should also notice the subtle but significant issue of capital and lower case letters in the spelling of God/gods. It has been a long-standing tradition in English Bibles to capitalize the word "God" when the word refers to the God of Israel, but to use lower case "g" when the word refers to a god or gods other than the God of Israel. By making this simple distinction, the English translator is also making an ultimate theological claim. However, the ancient languages that are dealt with in this study did not have capital and lower case letters, so the distinction in English usage between God(s) and god(s) was not marked.

Ancient Versions

We turn now to the ancient translations (also called "the versions") of Psalm 29. The left-hand column below contains the author's wooden English translation of the Hebrew. Then in sequence follow the author's translations of the Aramaic, Greek, Old Latin and Saint Jerome's Latin versions. The reader should be aware of the unique case of the Old Latin, since this translation was made from the Greek version and not directly from Hebrew. It is therefore called a translation "twice removed." The three other versions were directly translated from Hebrew.

Hebrew	Aramaic	Greek	Old Latin	Jerome's Latin
1 A psalm of David	A praise song of David	A psalm of David of the final day of (the Feast of) Tabernacles.	A psalm of David on the final day of (the Feast of) Tabernacles.	A canticle of David.
Ascribe to YHWH,	Ascribe before YHWH a praise song,	Bring to the Lord	Bring to the Lord,	Bring to the Lord
O sons of (the) G(g)od(s), ascribe to YHWH	O bands of angels, ascribe before YHWH	O sons of God, bring to the Lord young rams, bring to the Lord	O sons of God, bring to the Lord young rams. Bring to the Lord	young rams, bring to the Lord
glory and strength.	glory and strength.	glory and honor.	glory and honor,	glory and empire,
2 Ascribe to YHWH the glory of his name, bow down to YHWH in holy splendor.	Ascribe before YHWH the glory of his name, bow down before YHWH in holy splendor.	Bring to the Lord the glory due his name, bow down to the Lord in his holy court.	bring to the Lord the glory due his name, worship the Lord in his holy court.	bring to the Lord the glory due his name, worship the Lord in holy beauty.
3 The voice of YHWH upon the waters, the God of glory thundered, YHWH upon mighty waters.	The voice of YHWH is heard upon the waters in the strength of his glory YHWH thundered upon mighty waters.	The voice of the Lord upon the waters, the God of glory thundered, the Lord upon mighty waters.	The voice of the Lord is upon the waters, the God of majesty does thunder, the Lord upon mighty waters.	The voice of the Lord is upon the waters, the God of glory does thunder, the Lord upon mighty waters.

Hebrew	Aramaic	Greek	Old Latin	Jerome's Latin
4 The voice of YHWH	The voice of YHWH is heard	The voice of the Lord	The voice of the Lord	The voice of the Lord
in strength, the voice of YHWH	in strength, the voice of YHWH is heard	in strength, the voice of the Lord	in strength, the voice of the Lord	in force, the voice of the Lord
in splendor	in splendor	in magnificence.	in magnificence.	in beauty.
5 The voice of YHWH breaking cedars, and	The voice of YHWH shattering the cedars, and the word of	The voice of the Lord, who shatters cedars, and	The voice of the Lord, who shatters cedars, and	The voice of the Lord who shatters cedars, and
YHWH shattered the cedars of Lebanon.	YHWH shattered the cedars of Lebanon.	the Lord will shatter the cedars of Lebanon.	the Lord will shatter the cedars of Lebanon.	the Lord will shatter the cedars of Lebanon.
6 He made Lebanon skip	He made them skip	And he will crush them, even Lebanon,	And he will crush them	And he will scatter them as if (He were) a
like a calf,	like a calf,	like a calf,	like a calf of Lebanon,	calf of Lebanon,
and Sirion	and the mountain that produces rotten fruits,	and the beloved one	and the beloved one	and Sarion
like a young wild ox.	like a young wild ox.	is like a young unicorn.	is like a young unicorn.	as if (He were) a young rhinoceros.
7 The voice of YHWH hewing flames of fire.	The voice of YHWH hewing flames of fire.	The voice of the Lord who hews a flame of fire.	The voice of the Lord, who hews a flame of fire.	The voice of the Lord dividing flames of fire.
8 The voice of YHWH will convulse the wilderness,	The voice of YHWH shaking the wilderness, the word of	The voice of the Lord who shakes the wilderness,	The voice of the Lord who shakes the wilderness,	The voice of the Lord
YHWH will convulse	YHWH shaking [the serpent that is in]	and the Lord will shake	and the Lord will disturb	brings into labor
the wilderness of Kadesh.	the wilderness of Rekam.	the wilderness of Kades.	the wilderness of Cades.	the wilderness of Cades.

Hebrew	Aramaic	Greek	Old Latin	Jerome's Latin
9 The voice of YHWH will bring hinds into labor	The voice of YHWH brings the hinds into labor,	The voice of the Lord, who strengthens hinds,	The voice of the Lord who strengthens deer,	The voice of the Lord brings hinds into labor,
and stripped forests bare,	and makes wet the beasts of the forest,	and he will uncover thickets,	and he will uncover thickets,	and uncovers forests,
and in his temple	and in his temple on high	and in his temple	and in his temple	and in his temple
all	all of his attendants	everyone	all	all
(are) saying "Glory."	say "Glory" before him.	says "Glory."	will say "Glory."	will speak "Glory."
10 YHWH sat	YHWH sat upon the thrones of judgment against the generation of the flood to punish them,	The Lord will cause	The Lord causes	The Lord inhabits
at the flood,		that which was flooded to be inhabited,	that which was flooded to be inhabited,	the flood,
and YHWH sat	and YHWH sat on the thrones of mercy and rescued Noah,	and the Lord sits	and the Lord will sit	and the Lord will sit
as king	and he is king over his sons	as king	as king	as king
forever.	forever and ever.	forever.	forever.	forever.
11 YHWH will give strength to his people, YHWH will bless his people with peace.	YHWH gave the Torah to his people, YHWH will bless his people with peace.	The Lord will give strength to his people, the Lord will bless his people with peace.	The Lord will give strength to his people, the Lord will bless his people with peace.	The Lord will give force to his people, the Lord will bless his people with peace.

By scanning the parallel columns one can see that the Aramaic is clearly periphrastic/expansive. In part the Aramaic translation provides its own commentary on the text, making clearer the meaning of the poem as understood by the translator. If this column were omitted the others would align very closely with the Hebrew column. Though the Aramaic column appears to be the most divergent, the other columns also manifest literally dozens of translational differences. Only a small sampling of these can be discussed here.

In the Greek and Old Latin of 29:1 a liturgical rubric associating Psalm 29 with the Jewish autumn festival of *Sukkot* (Booths/Tabernacles) is preserved. Rabbinic sources also associate the psalm with this festival as well as with *Rosh Hashanah* (New Year's Day) and with the prayer for rain in the daily liturgy. Such liturgical rubrics are fairly common in the Greek Psalter and often provide helpful historical data for reconstructing Jewish liturgical practice in the Second Temple (i.e., post-biblical) period.

The Greek and both Latin versions render the tetragram with the generic word for "lord," *kurios* and *dominus* respectively, reflecting and accepting the contemporary standard Jewish practice. This move takes place throughout the Greek and Latin Bibles and is not at all restricted to this particular psalm. In so doing, however, an ambiguity is set up. If one only had the Greek or Latin text one would have no idea whether the original Hebrew used YHWH or *'adonay*, and thus a clear distinction in the Hebrew has been lost. On the other hand, this would prove to be of immense significance for Christian interpreters because *kurios* and *dominus* also happen to be the most common title ascribed to Jesus Christ in Greek and Latin Christianity.

The problematic Hebrew phrase "sons of (the) G(g)od(s)" produces a dynamic reaction in all of the versions. Greek and Old Latin entirely eliminate the ambiguity in "G(g)od(s)" (*'elim*) by rendering it emphatically in the singular: God. "Sons," however, remains plural. The result seems to be that the existence of lesser divine beings (perhaps angels) is allowed, but it clarifies that there is one and only one chief divine being to which these are subject. The Aramaic "bands of angels" is striking. On the one hand it accepts the Hebrew "G(g)od(s)" or "divine beings" as a genuine plural form, but then renders this plurality not as "Gods" or "divine beings" but specifically as "angels" thus eliminating any explicit divine reference.

The Greek and Latin versions highlight still another problem with the Hebrew word *'elim*. The Hebrew language has a word that sounds exactly like *'elim*, but which is written slightly differently (*'eylim*) and means "rams." Thus, the phrase "sons of G(g)od(s)" and "sons of rams" would sound exactly the same in Hebrew, but with a one-letter difference in spelling. This alternative reading is reflected in St. Jerome's Latin where the vocative, "Oh sons of G(g)od(s)," simply becomes the direct object, "sons of rams" (i.e., "young rams"). This reading also occurs in some medieval Hebrew manuscripts.

The Greek and Old Latin versions also reflect a phenomenon called double translation. This is when two different translations of a word or phrase are allowed to stand side by side. Instead of choosing one translational possibility over another, both possibilities are allowed to stand. Thus: "Bring to the Lord, O sons of God, bring to the Lord young rams."

Four verses (5, 7, 8, 9) contain the phrase, "The voice of the Lord," and are then immediately followed by an action. The Greek and Latin versions clarify a subtle ambiguity in the Hebrew, such that it is the Lord who is explicitly the actor rather than the Lord's voice. Thus, the translations consistently read, "The voice of the Lord who . . ." and not "The voice of the Lord which . . ."

On strictly grammatical grounds 29:6 is the most difficult in the psalm and this accounts for much of the variation in the versions. In addition the rare Hebrew word *Sirion* proved to be puzzling to the translators. Its only other occurrence in the Bible is in Deut 3:9, where it is a reference to Mt. Hermon (on the southern end of the anti-Lebanon range, north of Israel). Rather than letting the word stand as a proper name, the Aramaic, Greek, and Old Latin apparently view *Sirion* as a kind of code-name and attempt to translate it: "the mountain that produces rotten fruits," "the beloved one." The latter of the two is the more intriguing. The Greek translator has apparently misread the Hebrew *Sirion* for another rare Hebrew word, *jeshurun*. Though hard to appreciate in English, in Hebrew the forms "*and Sirion*" and "*jeshurun*" look very similar. The obscure *jeshurun*, perhaps an honorific title for Israel, only occurs in Deut 32:15; 33:5, 26; and Isa 44:2. In all of these instances the Greek translator renders *jeshurun* with "the beloved one," just as happens in this verse. But what is this translation supposed to mean here? It is impossible to be certain, but minimally one could say that a perceptive Jewish reader would have seen here a reference to Israel while a perceptive Christian reader would have seen a veiled prophetic reference to "the beloved one" of the New Testament.

Of all the versions, St. Jerome's Latin is the closest to the Hebrew, but with a twist. For Jerome it is the Lord himself whose actions are compared to those of a calf and a young rhinoceros. Though strange at first sight, see Num 23:22; 24:8; and Deut 33:17 as passages that may have influenced Jerome's thinking on this verse. The Hebrew *re'em* clearly designated a horned animal, now generally agreed to be a wild ox, but the multiple references to the horns of these animals (Num 23:22; Ps 22:21) appears to have caused translators of the Greek and Latin communities to assume that the marvelous nature of the horn defined the animal; hence, in the Septuagint and Old Latin versions it became a "unicorn," a fabulous, but none-the-less believed in, animal, and Jerome translated the term as referring to the rhinoceros, believed by some in the Roman world at the time to be the fabled unicorn.

The Greek and Latin versions are noteworthy in regard to the verbal tense of verses 5 and 6. The Hebrew and Aramaic are most naturally read as providing a retrospective on God's past action, whereas the Greek and Latin read the verses as prospective: God's shattering, scattering, and crushing activity still awaits its fulfillment in the future. Though the book of Psalms is not a prophetic book *per se*, later translators in Jewish and Christian traditions that accepted David as a poet-prophet saw the psalms as virtually saturated with prophetic passages. This is likely one such example.

The precise translation and meaning of the terse verse 29:10 is highly elusive and this is reflected in the versions. The Hebrew phrase which I have rendered as "at the flood" could as well be rendered "on/upon/over/above/from/for the flood;" all of which suggest slightly different nuances. In addition, the very meaning of the Hebrew word for flood, *mabbul*, is not clear. Which *mabbul* is being referred to here? Apart from Psalm 29, the actual Hebrew word *mabbul* occurs only in Genesis and there it is always a reference to Noah's flood. The Aramaic makes this identification specific. But the Psalter also knows of other "floods," like the primordial chaotic waters subdued by God (Ps 74:12–17) or the celestial waters above the dome of the sky which God holds at bay, both of which are highly positive images in the sense that God is the controller or restrainer of the flood rather than the one who brings it.

Greek and Old Latin seem to concur with the Aramaic in understanding the flood as Noah's flood, but the problem is complicated by the sense of the Hebrew verb *yashav*, here translated in the past tense as "sat." The verb allows various meanings: sit/dwell/inhabit/live, but also sit (on a throne), which is clearly indicated in the second half of the verse. If so, this raises the question of how God's "kingly sitting" is to be related to such a horrific event as Noah's flood. The Aramaic version saw the problem and solved it by interpreting God's kingly sitting in a dual fashion: as the exercise of both judgment and mercy. The solution adopted by the Greek translator, and followed by the Old Latin, involves reading the Hebrew verb "to sit/inhabit" as a transitive rather than an intransitive verbal form: "cause to be inhabited." This is an unlikely, but nevertheless possible, reading of the consonantal Hebrew text. The result is that the Greek and Old Latin emphasize not God's destructive activity in *de*populating the earth by means of the flood, but rather God's constructive activity in *re*populating the earth after the flood. If the received Greek text can be trusted at this point (there is a question as to the correctness of the Greek verb here translated "cause to be inhabited"), this would be an example of a rather exquisite theological interpretation.

Early Modern and Modern Versions

We turn finally, and only briefly, to a selection of prominent early-modern and modern translations of the psalm. The Luther Bible of 1545 and the King James Version (KJV) of 1611 were the most influential translations to emerge from the period of the Reformation and its immediate aftermath. The New Jewish Publication Society translation of 1985 (NJPS) and the New Revised Standard Version of 1989 (NRSV) represent two of the most popular contemporary translations from the Jewish and Christian communities respectively. These versions, all four of which were produced by committees or teams, are direct translations from the Hebrew, with the latter two reflecting engagement with modern philological and critical scholarship. The wooden Hebrew translation is once again provided in the first column for purposes of comparison.

Adapting Psalm 29 through Translation

Hebrew	Luther's Bible	KJV	NRSV	NJPS
1 A psalm of David. Ascribe to YHWH, O sons of (the) G(g)od(s), ascribe to YHWH glory and strength.	A psalm of David. Bring to the LORD O you mighty ones, bring to the LORD honor and strength.	A Psalm of David. Give unto the LORD, O ye mighty, give unto the LORD glory and strength.	A Psalm of David. Ascribe to the LORD, O heavenly beings, ascribe to the LORD glory and strength.	A psalm of David. Ascribe to the LORD, O divine beings, ascribe to the LORD glory and strength.
2 Ascribe to YHWH the glory of his name, bow down to YHWH in holy splendor.	Bring to the LORD the honor of his name; pray to the LORD in holy attire.	Give unto the LORD the glory due unto his name; worship the LORD in the beauty of holiness.	Ascribe to the LORD the glory of his name; worship the LORD in holy splendor.	Ascribe to the LORD the glory of His name; bow down to the LORD, magestic in holiness.
3 The voice of YHWH upon the waters, the Go of glory thundered, YHWH upon mighty waters.	The voice of the LORD blows upon the waters; the God of honor thunders, is upon the mighty waters.	The voice of the LORD *is* upon the waters; the God of glory thundereth; the LORD *is* upon many waters.	The voice of the LORD is over the waters; the God of glory thunders, the LORD over mighty waters.	The voice of the LORD is over the waters; the God of glory thunders, the LORD over the mighty waters.
4 The voice of YHWH in strength; the voice of YHWH in splendor	The voice of the LORD blows with might; the voice of the LORD blows marvelously.	The voice of the LORD *is* powerful; the voice of the LORD *is* full of majesty.	The voice of the LORD is powerful; the voice of the LORD is full of majesty.	The voice of the LORD is power; the voice of the LORD is majesty;
5 The voice of YHWH breaking cedars, and YHWH shattered the cedars of Lebanon.	The voice of the LORD breaks the cedars; the Lord breaks the cedars in Lebanon	The voice of the LORD breaketh the cedars; yea, the LORD breaketh the cedars of Lebanon.	The voice of the LORD breaks the cedars; the LORD breaks the cedars of Lebabon.	The voice of the LORD breaks cedars; the LORD shatters cedars of Lebanon.

Hebrew	Luther's Bible	KJV	NRSV	NJPS
6 He made Lebanon skip like a calf,	and makes them balk like a calf, Lebanon	He maketh them also to skip like a calf; Lebanon	He makes Lebanon skip like a calf,	He makes Lebanon skip like a calf,
and Sirion like a young wild ox.	and Sirion like a young unicorn.	and Sirion like a young unicorn.	and Sirion like a young wild ox.	Sirion like a young wild ox.
7 The voice of YHWH hewing flames of fire.	The voice of the LORD hews like flames of fire.	The voice of the LORD divideth the flames of fire.	The voice of the LORD flashes forth flames of fire.	The voice of the LORD kindles flames of fire;
8 The voice of YHWH will convulse the wilderness,	The voice of the LORD agitates the wilderness; the voice of	The voice of the LORD shaketh the wilderness;	The voice of the LORD shakes the wilderness;	the voice of the LORD convulses the wilderness;
YHWH will convulse the wilderness of Kadesh.	the LORD agitates the wilderness of Kadesh.	the LORD shaketh the wilderness of Kadesh.	the LORD shakes the wilderness of Kadesh.	the LORD convulses the wilderness of Kadesh;
9 The voice of YHWH will bring hinds into labor and stripped forests bare, and in his temple all (are) saying "Glory."	The voice of the LORD agitates the hinds and strips the forests bare. And in his temple all will speak honor to him.	The voice of the LORD maketh the hinds to calve, and discovereth the forests; and in his temple doth every one speak of *his* glory.	The voice of the LORD causes the oaks to whirl, and strips the forest bare; and in his temple all say, "Glory!"	The voice of the LORD causes hinds to calve, and strips forsests bare; while in His temple all say "Glory!"
10 YHWH sat at the flood, and YHWH sat as king forever.	The LORD sits, to prepare a flood. And the LORD remains a king forever.	The LORD sitteth upon the flood; yea, the LORD sitteth King for ever.	The LORD sits enthroned over the flood; the LORD sits enthroned as king forever.	The LORD sat enthroned at the Flood; the LORD sits enthroned, king forever.

Hebrew	Luther's Bible	KJV	NRSV	NJPS
11 YHWH	The LORD	The LORD	May the LORD	May the Lord
will give	will give	will give	give	grant
strength	strength	strength	strength	strength
to his people,	to his people;	unto his people;	to his people!	to His people;
YHWH	the LORD	the LORD	May the LORD	may the LORD
will bless	will bless	will bless	bless	bestow
his people	his people	his people	his people	on His people
with peace.	with peace.	with peace.	with peace!	wellbeing.

The reader will notice the striking similarity among the respective columns. Certain stylistic differences are apparent, especially in the German Luther Bible, but overall these versions understand the psalm in nearly identical fashion. To a large extent this reflects the common understanding among Protestants that the original Hebrew text is the authoritative biblical word of God and so all translators began with the Hebrew text itself. Nevertheless, 29:1 merits our attention. Immediately noticeable is the visual representation of the tetragram. It was the decision of the translators of the Luther German Bible to render the tetragram with all capital letters (HERR = LORD), thus making it possible even in translation to recognize the Hebrew Bible's distinction between YHWH and 'adonay. The overwhelming majority of Bible translations since then have adopted the same practice, as is evident here in all of the English translations, Christian or Jewish. To this author's knowledge, it is only the Jerusalem Bible and the New Jerusalem Bible which adopt the practice of rendering the tetragram according to the modern scholarly reconstructed form, Yahweh. The ancient Jewish tradition, concretely reflected in the translational practice of the Greek Bible, to avoid pronunciation of the divine name, continues to this day as the standard practice of Christian Bible translators as well.

The knotty Hebrew phrase, *beney 'elim*, "O sons of (the) G(g)od(s)," continues to cause problems for translators. Though the choices adopted by the Luther Bible and the KJV, "O you mighty ones"/"O ye mighty," are indeed possible translations of the Hebrew; both have to be regarded as theologically motivated evasions which eliminate the provocative ambiguity in the original. This ambiguity, however, is preserved in the subtle renderings of the NRSV and the NJPS: "O heavenly beings" / "O divine beings." In order better to appreciate the difficulties faced by translators of Psalm 29:1, those so motivated are encouraged to do their own comparative work on similarly problematic texts such as Exod 15:11, Ps 82:1, Job 1:6, and Job 2:1. Placing side by side various English translations of these texts will yield fascinating insights.

This exercise has highlighted a small selection of significant translational/interpretive issues involved in rendering the Hebrew text of Psalm 29 into other languages. The attentive reader will undoubtedly notice and discover many others. At the very least, however, it should be clear that translating Psalm 29 through time and various traditions entails interpreting the text and embodying commentary into the translations themselves.

Bibliography

Alexander, Philip S. "Targum, Targumim." In *ABD* 6:320–31.
Alter, Robert. *The Book of Psalms: A Translation with Commentary*. New York: Norton, 2007.
Birdsall, J. Neville. "Versions, Ancient (Survey)." In *ABD* 6:787–93.
Bogaert, Pierre-Maurice. "Versions, Ancient (Latin Versions)." In *ABD* 6:799–803
Greenspoon, Leonard J. "Versions, Ancient (Greek Versions)." In *ABD* 6:793–94.
Handy, Lowell K. *Among the Host of Heaven: The Syro-Palestinian Pantheon as Bureaucracy*. Winona Lake, IN: Eisenbrauns, 1994.
———. "One Problem Involved in Translating to Meaning: An Example of Acknowledging Time and Tradition." *SJOT* 10 (1996) 16–27.
Martin, Rose. "Names of God in the Old Testament." In *ABD* 4:1001–11.
Nida, Eugene A. "Theories of Translation." In *ABD* 6:512–15.
Pardee, Dennis. "On Psalm 29: Structure and Meaning." In *The Book of Psalms: Composition and Reception*, edited by Peter W. Flint and Patrick D. Miller, Jr., 153–83. VTSup 99. FIOTL 4. Leiden: Brill, 2005.
Stec, David M. *The Targum of Psalms*. ArBib 16. Collegeville, MN: Liturgical, 2004.

3

Echoes of "the Voice"
Psalm 29 in the Fathers

Jeffrey B. Gibson

I STATE AT THE OUTSET THAT I HAVE, FOR SOME TIME NOW, BEEN approaching the topic assigned me with fear and trembling. I confess straightaway, since it would soon become apparent in due course anyway, that, like Ben Johnson with respect to ancient languages, I have little grounding in the writings of the Fathers and even less in the ins and outs of their use of scriptural texts. Indeed my sense of trepidation over being able to do justice to my assignment lay hard upon me from the first day I began to work on the topic at hand when, thinking it wise as a stepping stone to be able to say anything at all on Psalm 29 in the Fathers of the Church. I first gave myself the task of becoming acquainted with what others have written on the Fathers' methods of interpretation and exegesis. I was increasingly struck by the realizations not only of how much material on the subject there is to digest, but of how little I understood even the small bit of it that time and other constraints permitted me to read. I have been aided immeasurably in writing the chapter by Larry Swain, doctoral candidate in Medieval Studies at the University of Illinois, and Chris Weimer, doctoral candidate in Classics at the University of Memphis, who provided translations of the Latin Fathers. So I emphasize that this chapter is a preliminary report on the use of Psalm 29 by the Fathers. All I will be doing here is to answer several very basic questions about the psalm and the Fathers that will provide data for those who wish to delve more deeply into the questions of the methods, aims and peculiarities of Patristic exegesis.

These questions are:

1. Who among the Fathers quotes the psalm and in which of their works?
2. How extensive is their quotation?
3. What according to the Fathers who quote the psalm, is the nature of the voice that is spoken of in Psalm 29?
4. If the voice is regarded as an utterance, who is it, according to each of the Fathers who quote the psalm, who stands behind the "voice" that the psalm celebrates?
5. On what occasion, according to the Fathers, does the "voice" sound out?
6. What are the "waters" upon which the voice "rests"?
7. Toward what end does the voice sound out?

Where Are Quotations of the Psalm to Be Found?

The "early Church Fathers" are here taken to mean those who wrote prior to the sixth century CE. Thus, significant expositions of Psalms by John of Damascus, Cassiodorus, Gregory the Great, and Bede are not taken into consideration here. The Greek Fathers who quote and/or use the psalm are Athanasius, Diodorus of Tarsus, Theodore of Mopsuetia, Basil of Caesarea, Cyril, Didymus Caecus, Ephraem, Eusebius, Gregory of Nyssa, Hippolytus, John Chrysostom, Oecumenius, Origen, Procopius, Severianus, and Theodoret of Cyrus. The Latin Fathers are Ambrose, Chromatius, Rufinus, Jerome, Augustine, Peter Chrysologus, Arnobius Junior, and Maximus of Turin.

Psalm 29, while not one of the most quoted of the psalms, appears many times in early church literature. Athanasius quotes or uses Ps 29 six times in his *Expositiones in Psalmos* (27.152.39, 49; 153.5, 9, 24, 34) and once in his *Quaestiones ad Antiochum ducem* (28.689.20) and once in his *Epistula ad Marcellinum de interpretatione Psalmorum* (27.13.16). Diodorus quotes it some twelve times in his *Commentari in Psalmos*; Theodore quotes it some six times in his *Expositio in Psalmos*. Basil quotes it twelve times in his *Homiles on the Psalms* (29.284.24; 288.38; 289.19, 39; 292.41; 293.26; 297.10, 36; 301.24, 30, 39; 304.48), in his *Psalmum* (30.73.28; 76.23, 36, 41; 77.23; 80.23), and in his

Homiliae in hexaemeron (6.3.19). Cyril cites it once in *Commentarius in Isaiam prophetam* (70.948.45), as does Didymus Caecus in *De trinitate* (39.681.30) and Ephraem in his *Sermo de Virtutibus Vitiis* (144 147.2). Eusebius quotes Ps 29 nine times in his *Commentaria in Psalmos* (23.252.8; 256.1, 15, 34; 257.9, 17, 18, 27, 30) and once in his *Commentarius in Isaiam* (1.62.30). Gregory of Nyssa cites it once in his *In diem luminum* (9.237), Hippolytus once in his *De theophania* (7.11) and John Chrysostom once in *In sanctam theophaniam seu baptismum Christi* (50.808.13). Origen quotes the psalm four times, three times in *Selecta in Psalmos (12.1289.42; 1292.1)* and once in *Fragmenta in Psalmos* (28.9.1). Theodoret has seven citations in his *Psalmos* (80.1064.21; 1065.5, 20, 36; 1068.12, 21; 1069.20).

In the Latin West Ambrose of Milan quotes Psalm 29 in chapter 12 of his *Apology for the Prophet David* (12.58–59) and in chapter 5 of *De Mysteriis*. Chromatius cites Ps 29 in chapter 3 of his *Tractatus on Evangelii S. Matthaei* (19 iii), Rufinus in his *Commentarius in LXX Psalmos* (Ps 28), Jerome in his *Breviarum in Psalmos* and his *Commentary on Isaiah*, Peter Chrysologus in his *Sermo CLX: De eisdem*, Arnobius Junior in his *Commentarii in Psalmos* (Ps 28), and Maximus of Turin in his *Sermones de Tempore* (Sermo X: De S. Epiphania iv). The most influential of all church Fathers, Augustine of Hippo deals with Ps 29 in his *Enarrationes in Psalmos* (Ps 28) and his *Sermones de Tempore* (Sermo CXXXVII).

The Extent of the Quotation

How extensive the quotation of the psalm is in any of the works depends largely on the nature of the work in which quotations from the psalm appear. If the work is a commentary or a sermon on the psalm itself, as is the case for example with Theodoret's *Interpretatio in Psalmos* or Augustine's *Enarrationes*, we find all of its verses referred to and discussed in some fashion. If the work is a sermon that was composed for a particular occasion within the festal calendar or a discourse on, or an exposition of, a matter of doctrine, or a commentary or exposition of a biblical book other than the Psalms, as is the case in Gregory of Nyssa's *In diem luminum*, Maximus of Turin's *SermoX: De S. Epiphania iv*, Peter Chrysologus' *De eidem*, Didymus Caecus' *De trinitate*, and Chromatius in his *Tractatus on Evangelii S. Matthaei*, the quotation is usually limited to one verse and that primarily is verse 3 of the psalm, that is taken

The Nature of the Voice

up as proof text for, or an illustration of, the doctrine or issue under discussion.

At the heart of Psalm 29 stands a series of declarations concerning a "voice." It is a voice which is "upon" (Greek: *epi*) and "over" the "waters" (Ps 29:3) and which reveals the glory of the God of Israel. It is "powerful" and "majestic" (verse 4). It breaks in pieces the cedars of Lebanon (verse 5); it hews out or divides flames of fire (verse 7) and shakes the wilderness (of Kadesh; verse 8). It makes the deer to calve, and strips the forests bare (verse 9).

It seems quite clear that the background of the language employed here is to be found in the language associated with Baal and his "holy voice" and that for the psalmist this "voice" was a thunderstorm in which the power and majesty of Yahweh as lord of nature manifests itself (Kraus 344–51; Craigie 245). But for the majority of the Fathers who quote Ps 29, the "voice" which the psalm celebrates is a *verbal utterance*. Only Diodorus, Theodore, Theodoret and Basil entertain the idea that "the voice" is, or might be, something other than spoken words. Basil notes that while there are grounds for taking it as a proclamation, it is more likely that it should be viewed as a great and terrifying noise. Diodorus and Theodore declare that "the voice" is a metaphor for the power that God displayed when, as reported in 2 Kgs 19:35–36, he sent his destroying angel to decimate the Assyrian army that during the reign of Hezekiah had been poised to attack Jerusalem. While concurring with both his Antiochene and non-Antiochene predecessors regarding the nature of "the voice," Theodoret goes beyond each of their views and asserts on the basis of the description in verse 5 of "the voice" as something that sounds out "in power" and "in majesty," that "the voice" mentioned in Psalm 29 has another referent as well, namely, the grace of the Spirit that at Pentecost filled "the apostles with power and might" and rendered "puny men magnificent."

How is this to be explained? In Basil's case it is because of an understanding on his part that Scripture should be used to interpret Scripture and that the meaning of words in any part of the biblical text is to be determined by the usage of those words elsewhere in Scripture:

> In many places you might find the word "voice" occurring. Therefore, for the sake of understanding what the voice of the Lord is, we should gather, as far as we are able, from the divine scripture what has been said about the voice; for instance, in the divine warning to Abraham: 'And immediately the voice came to him: He shall not be your heir . . .' And in Moses: "And all the people saw the voice and the flames . . .' Again, in Isaiah: 'The voice of one saying: Cry . . .' With us, then, voice is either air which has been struck [i.e. thunder] or some form which is in the air against which he who is crying out wishes to strike. Now, what is the voice of the Lord? Would it be considered the impact on the air? Or air, which has been struck reaching the hearing of him to whom the voice comes?

In Diodorus's and Theodore's case, it is because of their assumption that the meaning of a given psalm could only be obtained by contextualizing it within the "historia" outlined in 1–2 Samuel and 1–2 Kings, and more particularly, that Psalm 29 is a prophecy ro retelling of the events recounted in 2 Kgs 19:35–36. In Theodoret's case, it is because of his belief that:

> On the one hand this Psalm fits the time of King Hezekiah. On the other hand, it is about the king of us all who eradicates the error of idolatry and who illuminates the economy with rays of divine knowledge

particularly when gentiles are converted to the Gospel and undergo baptism at the hands of those "modern" sons of God who, in the tradition of the "sons of God" spoken of in Ps 29:1, which is to say: the apostles, who began to fulfill their commission given them by Jesus to bring to the Lord "the sons of rams," that is to say: the gentiles, after they had been filled by the power of the Holy Spirit at Pentecost to "go and baptize" the nations.

The Author of the Voice

As one would expect, given the explicit identification in verse 3 and elsewhere within the pslam of this "voice" as the voice of "the Lord," we should hardly be surprised to find that all the Fathers, both those writing in Greek from the East and those writing in Latin from the West, would assume or declare that the author of the voice is none other than the God of Israel. Nor would we be surprised, given both (a) when the

Fathers who quote the psalm wrote and (b) the fact that they are all in one way or another trinitarians, if not in fact ardent adherents of Nicean creedal formulations of this doctrine, that they would speak of the author of the voice as "the Father."

And this they do with two exceptions: Augustine and (with some reservation) Basil. Both Augustine and Basil identify the author of the voice as *Jesus*. Augustine does this on the basis of his view not only that Jesus was the subject of the Psalms, but that Jesus was *the true David as well as "Lord."* In other words, the entirety of the Psalter is not only Christ-centered, but *Christ-authored* (Byassee 54–96). Thus, for Augustine the references in Psalm 29 to the "voice of the Lord" are to be read as "the Voice of Christ." That Augustine's Trinitarian theology posits that anthropomorphic references to God in the Bible are references to Jesus as the Christ would also make a human voice for God the voice of Christ.

Basil sees Jesus as the author of the voice spoken of in Psalm 29 on the basis of (a) an understanding that the "many waters" over which Psalm 29 says the "voice of the Lord" sounds are "those made holy by [Christian] baptism" and (b) his belief that in commissioning his disciples to "Go . . . baptize in the name of the Father, and of the Son, and of the Holy Spirit," Jesus left behind a "voice" that was to be sounded out upon the waters in which catechumenates immersed themselves when they underwent baptism.

> Perhaps, even in a more mystic manner the voice of the Lord was upon the waters when a voice from above came to Jesus as he was baptized. "This is my beloved Son." At that time, truly the Lord [Jesus] was upon many waters, making the waters holy through baptism: but, the God of majesty thundered from above with a mighty voice of testimony. And over those to be baptized a voice left behind by the Lord is to be pronounced: "Go, therefore," it says, "baptize in the name of the Father, and of the Son, and of the Holy Spirit." Therefore, "the voice of the Lord is upon the waters."

On What Occasion Does the Voice Sound Out?

For reasons of space I limit my focus to what the Fathers say regarding "the voice" spoken of in verse 3. Most of the Fathers who quote the psalm note or assume what we have just seen Basil attest to: that the voice spoken of in this verse was that which the Synoptic evangelists tell us was sounded out at Jesus' baptism (Matt 3:13–17; Mark 1:9–11; Luke 3:21–22). That is to say, the "voice of the Lord" is the divine declaration that Jesus was God's beloved and favored son that, according to the evangelists, was heard when, immediately after Jesus' immersion by John the Baptist in the Jordan River, the heavens were opened and the Spirit descended upon him. The reason for this is not only that they found in the Synoptic accounts of Jesus' baptism language and themes that are highly reminiscent of the language and themes of Psalm 29, a heavenly voice sounding out over (and upon one in) waters, but because of a shared general hermeneutical assumption that the Psalms are at the very least, if not primarily, prophetic. In them one finds prefigurements of the life of Jesus. We see this plainly, for instance in Gregory of Nyssa's remark that "in writing in his book that passage . . . The voice of the Lord is upon the waters, the voice of the Lord in majesty," the "inspired David" was "foretelling also the voice which the Father uttered from heaven upon the Son at his baptism."

Moreover, there is also the fact that the declaration within the psalm regarding the might and majesty of the voice "fits" with certain theological assumptions about the significance of Jesus' baptism which, among a number of the Eastern Fathers, was viewed as the occasion both of a cosmically regenerating and renewing theophania, and, for the believer, of the reception of the power of the "sacrament" of baptism which Jesus' baptism initiated. As Hippolytus notes

> The beloved generates love, and the light immaterial the light inaccessible? This is my beloved Son." He who, being manifested on earth and yet unseparated from the Father's bosom, was manifested, and yet did not appear. For the appearing is a different thing, since in appearance the baptizer here is superior to the baptized. For this reason did the Father send down the Holy Spirit from heaven upon him who was baptized. For as in the ark of Noah the love of God toward man is signified by the dove, so also now the Spirit, descending in the form of a dove, bearing as it were the fruit of the olive, rested on him to whom the witness was borne. For what reason? That the faithfulness of the Father's voice might be made known and that the prophetic utterance of a long time past might be ratified. And what utterance is this? . . . "The voice of the Lord on the waters, the God of

glory thundered; the Lord upon many waters." And what voice? "This is my beloved Son, in whom I am well pleased." This is he who is named the son of Joseph and (who is) according to the divine essence my Only-begotten. "This is my beloved Son"— He who is hungry and yet maintains myriads; who is weary, and yet gives rest to the weary; who has not where to lay his head, and yet bears up all things in his hand; who suffers, and yet heals sufferings; who is smitten, and yet confers liberty on the world; who is pierced in the side, and yet repairs the side of Adam. (*De theophania* 7.11)

And Ambrose:

Why do you marvel if you see the sacraments of baptism? When [David] said above, where he describes the Passion of the Lord, the Lord feeds me, and nothing is wanting for me: in the verdant place there he lays me down, out of the water of refreshment he leads me (Ps. 22.2). And in another place: The voice of the Lord over the waters, the God of majesty thunders. (*Apology for the Prophet David*, ch. 12)

Is it not that you ought to doubt [that Christ is present in baptism], when clearly the Father calls to you in the Gospel who says, "Here is my Son in whom I am pleased; the Son calls, on whom also the Holy Spirit descended as a dove, and the Spirit itself calls who descended as a dove; David calls, "The voice of the Lord on many waters, the God of majesty thunders, the Lord over many waters." (*De Mysteriis*, ch. 5)

But there are exceptions to this view. There is, as should be expected, Augustine, who, as we have seen, regards the psalm as something spoken by *Jesus himself about himself and the nature and aim of his activity in the world* during his ministry. And there are, as we have also already seen, the Antiochene exegetes Diodorus and Theodore, who, while accepting that the voice is the voice of God, declare that the occasion for its sounding was God's rout of the siege made by the Assyrian king Sennacharib against Hezekiah's Jerusalem.

What Are the "Waters" upon which the Voice Sounds?

With respect to the question of the nature of the "waters" spoken of in Psalm 29, the Fathers are divided, with some overlap, into six camps. According to the Fathers, the waters represent:

1. The Jordan River in which Jesus was baptized (Theodoret, *Commentary* on Ps 29:3).
2. The water with which catechumenates are baptized.
3. The Gentiles who are brought by the preaching of the disciples and their successors into baptism.
4. The "saints" from within whom, in fulfillment of John 7:38, "rivers (that is: spiritual teaching which refreshes the souls of the hearers) flow.
5. The church (Augustine, beginning of comments on Psalm 29)
6. The hordes of the Assyrians spoken of in 2 Kings 19.

Who among the Fathers stands where is largely dependent upon what the nature and who the author of the voice is thought to be and what the Father envisages as the occasion in which the voice sounds out.

To What End Does the "Voice" Sound Out?

Here too Patristic views are varied. Many Fathers say, along with Ambrose, that the purpose of the voice sounding out is to show that baptism is fully efficacious in the removal of sin and that Christ is fully present in the sacrament. But Chromatius says that it has another aim: to confirm that the Old Testament points to Jesus and that in him prophecy is fulfilled. Theodore and Diodorus note that it was to rout the forces of Sennacherib and to demonstrate God's faithfulness to his promise to shield and save from any siege that the Assyrian king intended to lay against Jerusalem. Theodoret claims that it was to sanctify not only the Jordan but all other waters used elsewhere to administer baptism as well as to prophesy "the power imparted to apostles at Pentecost to preach salvation to the nations and offer those delivered by the Gospel message from idols to God." And Augustine declares that it is to demonstrate that the church is being perfected in this world and is the divine instrument through which Jesus displays his divinity.

Final Observations

I mentioned at the outset that I have little competence in matters Patristic, let alone the field of Patristic hermeneutical approaches to, and interpretation of, Scripture. So I am loathe to offer any conclusions about what is indicated by way of the methods, aims and peculiarities of Patristic exegesis from what I have outlined above. However, two things seem to be clear:

1. All of the Fathers, even those from schools of exegesis that stress examining the original/historical context of a text as a proper methodology for gaining a sound understanding of that text, work from an unquestioned assumption that biblical texts are alive. That is to say: biblical texts have a meaning that is relevant for, and which speaks to, their own times.

2. The explanation of the first observation is that no early church Father in either the East or West ever thought that the ultimate aim of biblical exegesis was anything other than a pastoral one or that it should ever be understood except to edify those for whom he wrote.

Whatever else may be derived from the data I have brought forward in the preceding pages I leave to the experts to adduce.

Appendix: A Verse-by-Verse Reading by Augustine of Psalm 29

Heading: The speaker ["David"] is Jesus concerning the perfection of the church in its struggle with the devil.

Verse 1: Using the Greek translation of "Bring to the Lord the offspring of rams," this is seen as a call for Christians to present themselves before God as the fruit of the preaching of the Apostles.

Verse 2: By glory and honor is meant the good works of the Christian. The glory of his name is a reference to the spreading of the Gospel through the world. One is to worship God in one's own heart is the interpretation of "in holy splendor."

Verse 3: The voice and the waters are the preaching of the word of God the Father by Jesus to the peoples who are struck by awe and convert.

Verse 4: Here the voice in strength is that word of God now residing in the believers.

Verse 5: Breaking cedars is the humbling of the proud, while the cedars of Lebanon are the most splendid and noble persons of this world being confounded by God who raises up the humble and brings down the mighty. Here Augustine contrasts Jews and Gentile Christians.

Verse 6: The reference to the calf is taken as a comment on Jesus' crucifixion at the hands of the powerful of this world. The Latin translation, from the Greek, has a unicorn for the second line and this is taken to be a reference to Jesus as the only beloved Son of God, who emptied himself of his glory to become human.

Verse 7: The voice cutting through fire is taken to be Christ passing safely through the conflicts and persecution to bring love to those who follow him.

Verse 8: The voice shaking the wilderness is the Gospel converting the Gentiles. Kadesh (which sounds like the Hebrew word for "holy") is understood to refer to the Holy Scriptures.

Verse 9: Using a translation with "perfecting the stags" this verse is understood as Jesus bringing correct understanding of the Scriptures, while in the church all are born again into eternal hope thereby praising the Holy Spirit for the gift of Christ.

Verse 10: The flood is taken as a reference to Noah's flood where God protected Noah, so God protects the Christians in this world and then will reign over them forever.

Verse 11: Strength will be given by God to withstand the turbulence of this world and in Christ will the Christian find peace.

Bibliography

Augustine. *Expositions of the Psalms, Volume 1:1–32*. Edited by John E. Rotelle; Translated by Maria Boulding. WSA 3.5. Hyde Park, NY: New City, 2000.

Blaising, Craig A., and Carmen S. Hardin, eds. *Psalms 1–50*. ACCSOT 7. Downers Grove, IL: InterVarsity, 2008.

Byassee, Jason. *Praise Seeking Understanding: Reading the Psalms with Augustine*. Grand Rapids: Eerdmans, 2007.

Craigie, Peter C. *Psalms 1–50*. WBC 19. Waco, TX: Word, 1983.

Hauser, Alan J., and Duane F. Watson, editors. *A History of Biblical Interpretation, Volume 1: The Ancient Period*. Grand Rapids: Eerdmans, 2003.

Kraus, Hans-Joachim. *Psalms 1–59: A Commentary*. Translated by H. C. Oswald. Continental Commentaries. Minneapolis: Augsburg, 1988.

Kugel, James L., and Rowan A. Greer. *Early Biblical Interpretation*. LEC 3. Philadelphia: Westminster, 1986.

Simonetti, Manlio, et al. *Biblical Interpretation in the Early Church: An Historical Introduction to Patristic Exegesis*. Edinburgh: T. & T. Clark, 1994.

4

Psalm 29 in Jewish Psalms Commentary (*Midrash Tehillim*)

King David's Instructions for Synagogue Prayer

Esther Menn *and* David Sandmel

JEWISH EXEGETICAL TRADITIONS ABOUT PSALM 29 SET FORTH IN *Midrash Tehillim*, the classic rabbinic commentary on the Psalms, suggest that one of King David's intentions as the author of this "Psalm of David" (Ps 29 superscription) was to anticipate the central daily prayer of rabbinic Judaism, commonly known as the Eighteen Benedictions. According to a line of interpretation forwarded in *Midrash Tehillim*, Psalm 29 presents David's programmatic structure for this synagogue prayer *par excellence*. While this understanding of Psalm 29 is clearly anachronistic, in that it attributes to the Israelite king detailed knowledge about a liturgical development dating to well over a millennium after his death, it does serve a strategic religious purpose. The presentation of Psalm 29 as David's own instructions concerning rabbinic prayer gives this innovation of the synagogue a prestige of ancient scriptural origins. This creative interpretation of Psalm 29 maintains a connection between the biblical heritage of the psalms, many of which were prayers and songs of praise for worship in the Jerusalem temple, and the new form of liturgy that emerged after the destruction of the temple in 70 CE.

Concerning the source of exegetical traditions explored here, the title *Midrash Tehillim* indicates that this medieval commentary contains "midrash," or rabbinic scriptural interpretation, on the book of "Praises" (*Tehillim*), as the book of Psalms is known in Hebrew. *Midrash Tehillim* is an extensive anthology, most likely compiled in either Palestine or some place in Europe in the eleventh to thirteenth centuries, although much material from earlier periods is incorporated. While the basic outline of synagogue worship was set well before the composition of *Midrash Tehillim* this commentary may nevertheless witness to some of the creative dynamics associated with the emergence of Jewish prayer. The rabbinic prayer of the synagogue linked to Psalm 29 in this commentary is known as the Eighteen Benedictions because of the original number of paragraphs offering praise, petition, and thanksgiving. (The name Eighteen Benedictions was retained even after a nineteenth benediction was added at some point, perhaps in the early centuries of the common era). It is also known by other names: Amidah or "standing" prayer named after the posture assumed to approach the heavenly king; and simply Tefillah, "the Prayer," because of its central importance. The Eighteen Benedictions are offered in some form (either full or abbreviated) at every synagogue service at least three times every day (Shaharit or morning prayer, literally "dawn," Minhah or afternoon prayer, literally, "offering," and the last to be added, Maariv or evening prayer, literally, "evening") in synagogues that follow traditional practice.

The structure of the synagogue prayer in its classic form opens with three benedictions praising God and closes with three benedictions thanking God. These may have been fixed first, with extemporaneous petitions offered between the introductory and concluding sections. In the weekday version there are thirteen petitions offered in between the opening blessings offering praise and the closing benedictions offering thanks. These petitions ask for the spiritual and physical needs of the individual members of the community (4–9) as well as of the entire community (10–15), followed by a concluding summary petition. On Sabbath, festivals, and the New Moon, the Amidah consists of the first three, last three, and an additional benediction appropriate for the day. This abbreviated form is known as the Seven Benedictions (with no petitions, since the joy of celebrating the Sabbath or a festival is incompatible with prayers that focus on what is lacking in the life of the individual and the community).

While *Midrash Tehillim* portrays the legendary origins of the Eighteen Benedictions in connection with Psalm 29, other rabbinic sources suggest that the historical origins of the Eighteen Benedictions were in the second temple period with further development in the centuries following the destruction of the temple in 70 CE.

In *Midrash Tehillim* a cluster of exegetical decisions concerning some of the puzzling features of Psalm 29 contribute to the larger interpretive project of identifying this Davidic psalm as an archetypal pattern for contemporary worship. Who are those being addressed in the first verse of this psalm, the *bene 'elim*, whom the NRSV translates as "heavenly beings" or "sons of gods" (Ps 29:1), but whom *Midrash Tehillim* understands very differently? What does it mean to "ascribe" (NRSV), or more literally to "give" to God such things as "glory and strength" (Ps 29:1), or "the glory of his Name" (Ps 29:2), since God already possesses all these attributes? What is the significance of the repetition of the Tetragrammaton (YHWH), God's holy proper name represented by "the LORD" in small capitals in the NRSV, throughout Psalm 29 a total of eighteen times?

In *Midrash Tehillim* 29.2 a lengthy passage connecting Psalm 29 and the Eighteen Benedictions is introduced in a commentary on the second verse of the psalm. What does it mean to "Ascribe to the LORD the glory of his Name" (Ps 29:2)? The interpretation of this repeated injunction is particularly revealing of the rabbis' perspective. The verb *habu*, literally "give," is a bit strange here linguistically, as well as the concept that one can contribute to the deity such things as glory and strength, which would seem to already be divine attributes. To answer the elusive problem of authorial intent regarding what this imperative might mean, in this commentary the figure of David himself makes a fortuitous appearance. This convention of a biblical worthy appearing to address the concerns of later Jewish communities is common in midrashic literature. Here *Midrash Tehillim* offers an interview with the author of Psalm 29 in an imaginative classroom setting. The dialogue reveals the concerns of the Jewish community and their teachers rather than anything about the historical David, of course, but the portrayal of David as teacher or rabbi is inspiring and revealing. David in *Midrash Tehillim* appears as a scholarly interpreter of the biblical writings, not one of his most noted roles in the Bible, but certainly in keeping with the high value placed on knowledge and learning by the sages in the rabbinic tradition.

In *Midrash Tehillim* 29.2 David explains that he had a liturgical intention in this "Psalm of David" to encourage the entire congregation of Israel to pray to God in response to his invocation of the divine Name. In writing Psalm 29 with its repeated invocation of the Divine Name, David meant to instruct all of Israel, meaning the entire Jewish community, to address God directly in prayer. In commenting on his own words in Ps 29:2, *Midrash Tehillim* reports David emphasizes his invocation of the name of God: "Ascribe to the LORD the glory of his Name" (Ps 29:2). "That is, whenever I (David) breathe his ineffable Name, you (plural, indicating all those reading and by extension the entire congregation of Israel) are to 'Ascribe to the LORD the glory of his Name.'"

The four-letter name of God, YHWH, appears centrally in Psalm 29 as well as in the midrashic treatment of this psalm. The name of God, revealed to Moses at the burning bush according to Exodus 3:15, so uniquely summarizes God's identity and power that in the course of time, out of respect and a sense of reverence, it ceased to be spoken, but instead the title of God, "Lord," was pronounced in its stead, a practice that continues to this day. The repeated mention of God's name in this psalm, a total of eighteen times, becomes a central feature of the midrashic interpretation that ensues.

The words that follow the quotation of Ps 29:2, which are entirely the creation of the midrashic imagination, begin to establish David as the patron and leader of Israel's prayer, which will ultimately be revealed as the Eighteen Benedictions through the course of the commentary on Psalm 29. They identify the action of "ascribing," or "giving," as liturgical in nature, as an antiphonal call and response across the millennia, initiated by David through his invocation of the holy name of the LORD and followed by the appropriate acknowledgment of God by the congregation.

The authority for the pattern that David provides in this psalm turns out to be even greater, as the traditional author of the Psalms himself validates his own interpretation of Psalm 29 by appealing to an even more ancient and authoritative figure from the tradition, namely Moses, the great prophet and lawgiver. This appeal to Moses follows a dynamic that may be seen throughout the pages of *Midrash Tehillim*, as well as in other rabbinic literature, in which David and Moses are often compared, with David always emerging as secondary to Moses. This weighing of the relative merit of these two biblical figures validates the community structures of Torah associated with Moses over the messianic and artistic traditions associated with David.

A citation of a verse from Moses' own magisterial poetic work in the Torah, the song in Deuteronomy 32, serves as an exegetical key. *Midrash Tehillim* 29.2 continues: "As Moses said, 'When I call on the Name of the LORD, ascribe greatness to our God'" (Deut 32:3; *Midrash Tehillim* 29.2). These two verses, David's "Ascribe to the LORD the glory of his Name," and Moses' "Whenever I call on the Name of the LORD, ascribe greatness for our God," provide a striking pair, replete with a number of similarities. One of the most obvious correspondences between the two verses brought together in this passage is, of course, the plural imperative to "ascribe" to the divinity (designated by the divine Name in Ps 29 and the phrase "our God" in Moses' song). In each case what is ascribed are attributes of eminence ("glory of his Name" Ps 29:2, "glory and strength," Ps 29:1, and "greatness," Deut 32:3). The similarity of expression leads to a natural association of these verses.

Another connection between the two verses is the reference in each to the Name of the LORD (YHWH). But listing common aspects does not entirely get at the dynamic aspect of this juxtaposition of verses. Moses' declaration, "Whenever I call upon the Name of the LORD," (Deut 32:3; NRSV: "For I will proclaim the Name of the LORD"), followed by an imperative to the Israelites to do the same, is given a distinctive sense in the commentary. These two phrases are not seen as two parallel parts of a single verse, both referring to praise of God by different parties, first Moses and then by the larger group. These two phrases are instead understood as a sequence, with the second action dependent on Moses' initiative in the first half, by interpreting the Hebrew particle *ki* not as indicating emphasis or consequence ("for" in the NRSV), but temporarily as "whenever": "Whenever I call upon the Name of the LORD."

The remainder of the verse, containing the somewhat unexpected plural imperative "ascribe" immediately preceding Moses' own song now emerges as a result of Moses' own calling on the LORD. The imperative "Ascribe greatness to our God" (Deut 32:3), therefore anticipates the response of the entire community following the Exodus from Egypt. Here Moses takes the initiative in invoking the divine Name (the Tetragrammaton) and the congregation is called upon to follow suit in acknowledging God's presence with the community through their direct address, adoringly ascribing to their God the attribute of greatness. "Whenever I call upon the Name of the LORD, you all should ascribe greatness for our God." Moses is initiating a call and response pattern, which suggests that David did the same in Psalm 29. At least that is how the midrashic David is justifying his own claim that his calling on the name of God in Psalm 29 is invoking a similar response from the Jewish community reading *Midrash Tehillim*.

While Ps 29:2 itself does not contain any explicit indication that David's invocation of the ineffable Name in Psalm 29 should inspire the community's direct address of the divinity, David's appeal to the Mosaic precedent in Deut 32:3 suggests that the same dialogic alternation between leader and community pertains equally to Psalm 29. To eliminate any doubt as to the nature of this call and response that David and Moses initiate in their respective cases, a simple gloss defines the meaning of "ascribing" attributes to the divinity, such as greatness (Deut 32:3), glory and strength (Ps 29:1), and the glory of his Name (Ps 29:2). *Midrash Tehillim* explains: "This (ascribing) means praying prayers before him (God)" (*Midrash Tehillim* 29.2).

Midrash Tehillim's interpretation of Psalm 29 therefore presents this psalm as David's repeated invocation of the divine Name, significantly a total of eighteen times, in order that all of Israel might offer their prayers to God in response. The nature of the prayer offered by the congregation is moreover not left unspecified in *Midrash Tehillim*, but rather is explicitly identified as the central prayer of the Jewish community through a lengthy section that correlates each mention of the divine Name in the psalm with one particular blessing from the Eighteen Benedictions. David's eighteen repeated utterances of the ineffable Name of God in Psalm 29, thereby, become an evocation of the corresponding blessings of the Amidah that recognizes the full range of God's power and concern.

The next exegetical question in this passage from *Midrash Tehillim* involves the identity of those instructed to "ascribe to the LORD the glory of his name" (Ps 29:2) through prayer. In the context of this discussion of direct human address of God, the *bene 'elim* or literally "sons of god(s)" in Ps 29:1 would most naturally be members of the Jewish congregation, not "heavenly beings" as in the NRSV, whether understood as minor gods of the pantheon or as angels sounding celestial tribute. In the covenantal imagery of the Hebrew Scriptures Israel is portrayed as God's son (for example, see Exod 4:22-23; Deut 8:5; Jer 31:9; Hos 11:1), and this relational sense of the human "sons" of a heavenly father may resonate here. A bit further on in this same section, however, in a discussion of the first benediction concerning the favor shown to the patriarchs, there is a more explicit indication that those summoned to pray are not the metaphorical sons of God, but rather the "sons of Abraham, Isaac and Jacob." This paraphrase implies that the three patriarchs are to be understood as the "great" ancestors (*'elim*) of the Jewish people. In this interpretation the entire Jewish community, or more literally its male members who form the minyan or prayer quorum, are enjoined to pray as the "sons of Abraham, Isaac, and Jacob."

A few additional words about the *bene 'elim* are in order, however, since the entire commentary on Ps 29:1 that immediately precedes the passage that is the main focus of attention here offers four different interpretations of this cryptic phrase sequentially, without any one of them emerging as definitive. None of the traditions presented in *Midrash Tehillim* identifies those being addressed in Psalm 29 as divine beings, but rather as different human parties, all of whom have experienced suffering. The first midrashic tradition identifies those addressed in Ps 29:1 as the children of Israel, who act as if they were dumb (*'illem*, a word that sounds very similar to the word for "gods," *'elim*, in keeping with the rabbis' frequent use of puns) and deaf in that they bear their oppression under the yoke of hostile nations without complaining. They are like God's servant in Isa 47:19. Although they would have every right to challenge God, they have chosen to remain silent in order to sanctify the divine Name through the suffering they receive for their faithfulness. A related tradition follows, identifying Abraham as a prime example of "mute" (*'illem*) suffering when he complied with God's command to sacrifice Isaac (Gen 22). Abraham did not object, even though he could have held God to his promise for the future: "my covenant I will establish with Isaac" (Gen 17:21). In consideration of his obedience, Abraham asks God to forgive his descendents when they sin in the future. The third interpretation identifies those addressed as the sons of the "mighty men of the land" (*'ele ha-'areṣ*; see Ezek 17:13) who were taken into exile by the Babylonian king Nebuchadnezzar. Finally, in the fourth interpretation, they are the sons or children who are ready to be sacrificed like rams (*'elim*), exemplified once again by Abraham and also by his son Isaac. One was willing to sacrifice and the other was willing to be sacrificed.

Note that in every case the *bene 'elim* are human beings and in particular exemplary members of Israel, especially those associated with innocent suffering, whether biblical figures such as Abraham and Isaac, the generation of the Babylonian Exile, or those of every time and place who do not avoid persecution for their faith. This emphasis on the suffering of those addressed in Psalm 29 according to *Midrash Tehillim* suggests the medieval context of the crusader period, during which Jewish communities in Europe experienced atrocities at the hands of Christian armies. The stress is on the faithfulness of revered biblical characters, and by extension of their descendents in the Jewish community, despite duress and suffering. The dynamics of Psalm 29 remain rooted in the relationship between God and Israel, and the action of ascribing or giving is something that human beings, as worshipers of God, do on earth below.

This sense continues to operate in the commentary on Psalm 29 in *Midrash Tehillim*, preparing the reader to identify those who "ascribe to the LORD" as the Jewish community, marked by silent suffering yet called on by David in Psalm 29 to praise of God through prayer, specifically through the Eighteen Blessings. This identification may have been enhanced by the recent suffering by the Jewish community inflicted by the crusaders or during other periods of Christian domination.

Midrash Tehillim confirms that the Eighteen Benedictions are intended as the main subject of the commentary on Psalm 29. In response to the question: "How do we know how many prayers we are to offer?" another question is asked: "How many times does the ineffable Name occur in this psalm?" "Eighteen times," is the answer, which evokes the following instructions, "You must therefore offer Eighteen Benedictions." The identification with the Amidah is made explicit based on the correspondence between the number of invocations of God's name by David in Psalm 29 and the number of benedictions in the prayer. This interest in numbers, evoking gematria (a rabbinic exegetical method based on number correlations) gives rise to the question of whether the number of times the divine name is mentioned is a fortunate accident or whether the Psalm was edited in this final version in the Masoretic text to ensure that there were eighteen occurrences. Already in the Greek translation of the Septuagint, which may have been completed before the common era, there are eighteen occurences of the title "Lord" used to translate the Tetragrammaton.

According to *Midrash Tehillim*, David anticipates and provides a blueprint for the Eighteen Benedictions by employing the Name eighteen times and by giving clues in Psalm 29 as to the content and order of the benedictions. A citation of an even more authoritative figure, Moses, clarifies the significance of David's invocation of the LORD's name for the practice of synagogue prayers as a kind of call and response.

(The interpretation of *Midrash Tehillim* 29.2 as David's own instructions concerning synagogue prayer takes the singular pronouns and verbal forms as referring to David as the traditional author of Psalm 29. This interpretation differs from the translation of William G. Braude, who identifies Moses as the anonymous teacher in this passage. Moses is explicitly named only in connection with the citation of Deut 32:3, however. According to the line of interpretation followed in this essay, David is the main speaker who appeals to Moses as an even more prestigious biblical authority, in order to establish the connection between Psalm 29 and the Eighteen Benedictions.)

The passage in Midrash Tehillim goes on to indicate briefly the specific connections of each benediction to specific lexical features of Psalm 29, as well as to other biblical passages, since most of the benedictions after the first three are primarily associated with verses outside of Psalm 29. The typical method of connecting the benedictions and Psalm 29, may be illustrated by the treatment of the first three benedictions, which are also linked with this psalm in the Talmud (*b. Megillah* 17b; *b. Rosh HaShanah* 32a). The Talmud does not explicitly connect the rest of the benedictions with Psalm 29; however, *Midrash Tehillim* may record a later stage in the development of a fixed order and content of the prayer than what is reflected in the Talmud.

The discussion of the Eighteen Benedictions one by one is introduced in *Midrash Tehillim* with yet another question, continuing the convention of a class in liturgy: "How do we know where to begin?" This question implies the need to provide a starting place for both the correspondence of Psalm 29 with the Eighteen Benedictions and, perhaps, for the sequential order of the benedictions themselves. The answer points to the first verse of the psalm: "Mark the beginning of the psalm: 'Ascribe to the LORD, sons of the mighty (*bene 'elim*)', that is 'sons of Abraham, Isaac and Jacob.' So you must say in the first benediction: 'The

God of Abraham, the God of Isaac, and the God of Jacob.'" Thus the first appearance of the name of the LORD in Psalm 29 stands for the first benediction, entitled *Avot*, or "Fathers." The full text of this opening benediction is not included in *Midrash Tehillim*, perhaps because it would have been so familiar. In its entirety it reads:

> Blessed are you, O LORD our God and God of our fathers, God of Abraham, God of Isaac, and God of Jacob, the great mighty and revered God, the most high God, who bestows loving-kindness, and is the Master of all things; who remembers the pious deeds of the patriarchs, and in love will bring a redeemer to their children's children for your Name's sake. O King, Helper, Savior and Shield. Blessed are You, O LORD, the Shield of Abraham.

According to the continuation in *Midrash Tehillim*, the second occurrence of the divine Name in Psalm 29, "Ascribe to the LORD glory and strength" (Ps 29:1) corresponds with the acknowledgment of God's glory and strength in the second benediction, known as *Gevurot*, or "Powers." This benediction includes a reference to the resurrection of the dead as the most powerful divine act. *Midrash Tehillim* states, "You must ascribe to Him glory and strength with, 'Blessed art you who revives the dead.'" The text of the entire second blessing is:

> You, O LORD, are mighty for ever, You revive the dead, You are mighty to save. You sustain the living with loving-kindness, revive the dead with great mercy, support the falling, heal the sick, free the bound, and keep faith with those who sleep in the dust. Who is like You, Lord of the mighty acts, and who resembles You, O King, who orders death and restores life, and causes salvation to spring forth? Yes, You are faithful to revive the dead. Blessed are you, O LORD, who revives the dead.

In *Midrash Tehillim* the third occurrence of the divine name, "Ascribe to the LORD the glory of his Name" (Ps 29:2a) corresponds to the third benediction, the sanctification of God's Name (*Kedushat haShem*). In the Talmud (*b. Megillah* 17b; *b. Rosh HaShanah* 32a) the entire second verse of Psalm 29, continuing with "Worship the LORD in the beauty of holiness" (Ps 29:2b), is associated with this third blessing in order to include the theme of "holiness." Because *Midrash Tehillim* takes as its project to associate each one of the eighteen appearances of the divine Name with one of the Eighteen Benedictions, it cannot include the reference to holiness in verse 2b, even though it would strengthen the correlation with the theme of the holiness of God's Name in the third benediction. To do so would set up two of the divine Names for a single blessing! This third benediction has a number of different formulations all of which feature the recitation of Isa 6:3, "Holy, holy, holy is the LORD of Hosts; the whole earth is full of his glory." The theme of "glory" is common to Isa 6:3 and Ps 29:2a, providing a verbal link between the biblical verse most directly associated with the third benediction and the phrase containing the third mention of the divine Name in Psalm 29.

As *Midrash Tehillim* continues, each of the remaining benedictions is correlated with an occurrence of the divine Name in Psalm 29 as they appear sequentially. There is a systematic working through the Eighteen Benedictions, in much the same order and with allusions to the same basic content as in the version still prayed today. The one exception is that the fifteenth benediction in the version of the Amidah used to this day, anticipating the coming of the Davidic messiah, is not explicitly cited in *Midrash Tehillim*. This missing blessing seems to be an additional variant of the messianic benediction concerning the God of David and the building of Jerusalem which appears in fourteenth place. At some point in time, two different versions of the messianic blessing were included, bringing the number of benedictions from eighteen to nineteen. *Midrash Tehillim* may refer to a form of the Eighteen Benedictions from before the time when both versions of the messianic blessing were included.

After the first three benedictions there is even less of an attempt to connect specific material in Psalm 29 with the content of each benediction in the Amidah. Rather, in most instances there are other biblical verses brought in which correspond to or further elucidate the particular blessing. In other cases, however, there are no biblical verses, but just a simple correlation between each phrase containing the Name of God in Psalm 29 and the next benediction in order through the Amidah. Clearly, there is an attempt to develop the tradition, stated more generally elsewhere, that the eighteen occurrences of the divine Name in Psalm 29 indicates the number of benedictions in the Amidah (*b. Berakot* 28b). The attempt is imposed and artificial; however, since in many cases the primary associations of the subsequent blessings lie elsewhere, in biblical passages with content more closely related to the specific benediction.

The overall effect of this interpretation is that the organic structure of Psalm 29, with its imagery of the effects of a storm representing the awesome power of God's appearance, is overwritten. It becomes a palimpsest, and what remains is no longer the structure of the poetry of Psalm 29 itself, but of the Eighteen Benedictions. The literal meaning of Psalm 29 is eclipsed so that the discussion of the psalm becomes in reality an overview of the central synagogue prayer. The multiple appearances of the Tetragrammaton become the primary focus as these become ciphers for the benedictions. This is an instance where scriptural interpretation effectively overwhelms and obscures the base in favor of foregrounding a later and more central religious manner of addressing God.

In the end, it is as if King David himself attended the first synagogue service ever held in order to instruct the congregation through his biblical composition on how to pray authentically. Through this midrashic interpretation a strange biblical composition urging the recognition of God's power, followed by the description of a theophany through the natural phenomena of a violent thunderstorm over ocean and through forests—more similar to what one might expect in the worship of a Canaanite deity such as Baal, with no mention of any distinctive themes of Israelite history or religion—is domesticated and transformed into the most compatible and even programmatic psalm, expressive of the contours of the contemporary rabbinic practice of daily prayer. According to *Midrash Tehillim*, David anticipated the needs of the congregation of Israel in rabbinic times, after the destruction of the temple, when new forms of worship were required. This foresight is all the more amazing in that he anticipated the needs of post-biblical synagogue worship even before the first temple had even been constructed! David's role in sponsoring prayer is a major theme throughout *Midrash Tehillim*, no doubt because this commentary treats the biblical book of Psalms as a collection of David's prayers, praises, laments, petitions and other addresses to God. The interpretation of Psalm 29 in *Midrash Tehillim* 29.2 as David's instructions for the Eighteen Benedictions provides a concrete illustration of his concern for Jewish prayer.

The Talmud points to alternative narratives concerning the origin of the Eighteen Benedictions. One rabbinic tradition asserts that the 120 elders of the Great Assembly, from the time of Ezra, composed the Eighteen Benedictions (*b. Megillah* 17b). Another tradition describes how Rabbi Gamaliel II led an initiative to fix the order of the Eighteen Benedictions after he destruction of the temple when many influential Jewish sages moved to a town named Yavneh on the Mediterranean coast (*b. Berakot* 28b; *b. Megillah* 17b). There was a controversy about this development, however, as other rabbis preferred the older custom of offering more extemporaneous forms of prayer (*b. Berakot* 28b). These traditions suggest that the Eighteen Benedictions had historical roots in the restoration period of the second temple and underwent further development even after the destruction of the temple in 70 CE. Yet, tracing the Eighteen Benedictions back to the Great Assembly or to a prestigious rabbi of the first century also imparts a legendary quality to their origins. The main difference between these traditions in the Talmud and the one in *Midrash Tehillim* concerning David is that in the latter case the founding figure is a biblical character. The origins of the Eighteen Benedictions have been pushed even farther back in sacred history, to the time of Israel's greatest king and model of biblical piety.

Attributing the structure of the central synagogue prayer to the biblical figure of David fits in with a larger project within rabbinic Judaism, that of linking the origins of post-biblical forms of piety with the ancient scriptural tradition. There are many other examples of this type of creative connection between biblical heritage and later religious practices. Keeping the focus on prayer, the rabbis portrayed the patriarchs Abraham, Isaac and Jacob as each instituting one of the three daily prayer services that ultimately became normative within Judaism (*y. Berakot* 4; *b. Berakot* 26b). According to this midrashic tradition, Scripture portrays Abraham offering the morning prayer when he "went early in the morning to the place where he had stood before the LORD" (Gen 19:27). For his part, Isaac established the late afternoon prayer when he "went out in the evening to walk in the field" (Gen 24:63). Since the word translated as "walk" may also mean "converse," the rabbis interpreted this verse to mean that Isaac was speaking with God in prayer. Finally, Jacob inaugurated the practice of evening prayer when he "came to a certain place and stayed there for the night, because the sun had set" (Gen 28:11); the narrative following this verse describes Jacob's direct encounter with God. One further example is the figure of Phineas, a zealous priest from the wilderness period (Num 25:6–13), who "stood up and interceded" with God to stop a plague (Ps 106:30). The midrashic interpretation of this verse in the Babylonian Talmud (*b. Berakot* 26b) attributes even the posture assumed in the Amidah ("standing") to ancient biblical precedent. Through midrash biblical worthies emerge as representatives of the continuity between an ancient scriptural past and the contemporary practices of rabbinic Judaism.

A more direct way of maintaining this continuity might have been simply to continue using the Psalms themselves as the central prayers of the synagogue. This was in fact the strategy of the Kairites, or literally "scriptural" Jews of the Middle Ages, who rejected rabbinic authority. This splinter group insisted that the Psalms themselves were the inspired liturgical prayers meant to be offered to God in Jewish worship throughout the ages. The Kairites regarded later rabbinic prayers and other elements of worship as intrusive innovations that should be abandoned in order to return to pristine biblical models. There is no explicit polemical tone or content in *Midrash Tehillim* that would suggest that its interpretation of Psalm 29 was directed against the Kairites. Yet, *Midrash Tehillim* and other rabbinic sources appear to both recognize the disjunction and innovation represented by the Eighteen Benedictions and yet also show a concern to maintain the connection with more ancient roots.

In conclusion, the commentary on Psalm 29 in *Midrash Tehillim* presents David as the traditional author of the Psalms legitimating an innovative form of prayer from the rabbinic period. Just as 1 Chr 28:11–19 portrays David as providing the divinely inspired blueprint for the temple that he himself did not build, so here David is depicted as anticipating details of Jewish liturgy that he did not live to see. This dynamic treatment of ancient Scripture negotiates a transformation in religious practice by portraying it in continuity with tradition. In *Midrash Tehillim* the ancient religious poetry of Psalm 29, which may be one of the oldest psalms in the Psalter, from the time of David or even earlier with Canaanite antecedents, points to the post-biblical development of the synagogue prayer. Psalm 29 not only retains its relevance, but even claims a foundational status in that it undergirds, legitimates and connects the worshiping community's recitation of the Eighteen Benedictions with an ancient biblical past. In *Midrash Tehillim*, David issues a call to the central rabbinic form of prayer across the centuries. To the modern eye this midrashic interpretation may appear anachronistic, unwarranted and at best whimsical, but its import is serious in that it validates a new form of contemporary piety (central synagogue prayer) forging a vital connection with the scriptural past.

Bibliography

Braude, William G., translator. *The Midrash on Psalms.* YJS 13. New Haven: Yale University Press, 1959.

Donin, Hayim Halevy. *To Pray as a Jew: A Guide to the Prayer Book and the Synagogue Service.* New York: Basic Books, 1980.

Elbogen, Ithamar. *Jewish Liturgy: A Comprehensive History.* Translated by Raymond P. Scheindlin. Philadelphia: Jewish Publication Society, 1993.

Epstein, I., ed. *The Babylonian Talmud.* London: Soncino, 1935–48.

Frishman, Elyse D., ed. *Mishkan T'filah: A Reform Siddur.* New York: Central Conference of American Rabbis, 2007.

Holliday, William L. *Psalms through Three Thousand Years: Prayerbook of a Cloud of Witnesses.* Minneapolis: Fortress, 1993.

Holtz, Barry W., ed. *Back to the Sources: Reading the Classic Jewish Texts.* New York: Simon & Schuster, 1984.

Idelsohn, A. Z. *Jewish Liturgy and Its Development.* New York: Dover, 1995.

Levi, Yitzhak. "Midrash Tehillim (Midrash Psalms)." In *EncJud* 11:1519–20.

Menn, Esther. "Praying King and Sanctuary of Prayer II: David's Deferment and Temple Dedication in Rabbinic Psalms Commentary (*Midrash Tehillim*)." *JJS* 53 (2002) 298–323.

———. "Sweet Singer of Israel: David and the Psalms in Early Judaism." In *Psalms in Community: Jewish and Christian Textual, Liturgical, and Artistic Traditions*, edited by Harold W. Attridge et al., 61–74. SBLSymS 25. Atlanta: Society of Biblical Literature, 2003.

Simon, Uriel. *Four Approaches to the Psalms: From Saadia Gaon to Abraham Ibn Ezra.* Translated by Lenn J. Schramm. Albany: State University of New York, 1991.

5

The Psalms and Psalm 29 among Syrian Christians

Paul S. Russell

MOST CHRISTIANS WHOSE COMMUNIONS SPRING FROM THE HOMELAND of Aramaic-speaking communities commonly use Syriac in their religious life while in daily life speaking other languages; some now use other languages for worship as well. To call these people "Syriac Christians" or "Syriac-Speaking Christians" would be somewhat inaccurate. "Syrian Christians" will be here used without intending to mean that they all come from the modern country of Syria, or attempting to take sides in the on-going debate about what these people ought to be called, or defining their true ethnic roots.

The Aramaic-speaking world knew the presence of Christians from the beginning of the church's life as the Acts of the Apostles tells us in its recounting of the miracle of Pentecost. This is an area that many westerners have not encountered before, so there is a need to orient ourselves to the way in which these people, so foreign to the modern west, thought and lived. This foreignness springs from the language barrier that existed between the Syriac-speaking church and the western Christian communities who communicated in Greek and Latin. Many Americans tend to think of languages as impassable barriers between people. This is not necessarily the case, but even if natives of areas with mixed cultures and ethnicities are granted more linguistic skills than general in America, it is true that languages control contacts between people and can form and restrict intellectual life (Russell, "Nisibis").

Syrian Christian literature suffered a much higher rate of loss and destruction than did those of their western brethren; however, enough material survives for us to hear some of their thoughts and concerns. They would be pleased at our making the effort to do so, for though modern universities commonly place the study of Syrian Christians in separate academic departments from the study of Greek and Latin communities, Syrian Christians did not desire to be separated from their fellows in faith. We know of long traditions of study and education designed to bridge the gap with the west, while the creation and persistence of the "schools" of Nisbis and Edessa (Becker) show their deep dedication to learning of all sorts.

Syrian Christians were and are not a unified body despite inhabiting the same vast swath of the earth's surface and sharing the same religious language. When the Church was rent by the Christological arguments that produced the early Ecumenical Councils, the Syrians found themselves divided into different groups out of communion with each other. Sometimes, as with the Christians of southern India, they had no knowledge of the quarrels that were taking place in the western church. During the sixth century Syrian Christianity included members of the Nicene Church in communion with Constantinople and the western churches, members of the Church of the East often called "Nestorian" or "Dyophysite" church, and members of the Syrian Orthodox Church also called "Jacobite" or "Henophysite." All Christians have suffered from division, but Syrians may have suffered the most since they have lived in close contact with each other and it was difficult for any group to hold their heads above the hostile floods that washed over them because of this sad rupturing of the unified church. Fortunately, they never completely ignored each other, remaining aware of the thoughts and writings of their separated brethren. This means that, although we have very little of the early works on Psalms that they actually produced, the little that we have connects us with the general thought of the Syrian Christians as they made use of each other's commentaries, sharing many of the same interpretive approaches.

The geographical spread of the Syrian language was always large enough to encompass more than one political state. In fact, their fervent missionary activity made the Syriac language churches the most widespread for many centuries. All of this expansion was achieved in the face of formidable obstacles of geography, politics, and cultural diversity.

Syrian Christians and their Cultural Homes

What were the difficulties that confronted them as they sought to make a place for themselves and their new religion? There were a number of things that were different for Christians in the Orient/Near East than for those in the Roman Empire:

1. The pagan cults that surrounded them and formed the religious expectations of their neighbors were often quite different than the classical Greek and Roman pantheons. In some ways they were more in tune with the paganism described in the Bible (Drijvers, Ross).

2. The presence and, beginning in the late fourth century, the resurgence of Zoroastrianism, the traditional religion of Persia, was a central element in the history and imagination of Syrian Christians. Even before the rise of Islam, Syrian Christians living under the sway of the Shah found themselves face to face with an organized, well-funded religious system that resisted them on theological, social and political grounds. The great persecutions of Christians by Zoroastrians began after the legalization of Christianity in the Roman world which has meant that it often is ignored completely in western courses on church history. The sheer numbers of Christians martyred in these onslaughts was much greater than those who suffered under pagan Rome (Moffett, Gilman and Klimkeit).

3. There was a more active and developed Jewish presence in Mesopotamia and the East than there was in most of the Roman world. This was the milieu that produced the great Babylonian Talmud and that sheltered the refugees fleeing from Roman oppression after the Jewish Revolt of 70 AD and the Bar Kokhba Rebellion of 150. The presence of Jewish learning and Bible scholarship in such profusion made it more influential among Syrian Christians than in the western church. This had an important effect on what Christians considered when they read Scripture and what tools they had to help them understand it (Chapin).

4. The education offered in the areas in which the Syrian Christians lived, stretching from the Mediterranean in the west to China in the east and south to Kerala, southern India, differed from that

influenced by Greek thought. While Greek education did cast its influence throughout the domains controlled by Alexander and his successors, that influence faded as one moved farther eastward and disappeared completely long before the farthest bounds of the spread of Syrian Christianity had been reached. This meant that other ways of thought played their part in forming the expression of Christianity in those regions.

5. Many Christians in the areas that used Syriac for its worship and religious writing lived in areas that never knew the comfort and security that came from membership in a legally established group. While persecution was not a constant reality for Syrian Christians outside the Roman umbrella, it was almost always a possibility. This sad situation continues to the present.

Syrian Christians and the Bible

The Bible most commonly used among Syrian Christians was called "the Peshitta," a name that means "simple" or "straightforward." This version was produced using the Hebrew Text as its basis, quite different from the Septuagint-centered Greeks to the west. The best recent study of the Old Testament of the Peshitta suggests that it had a "non-Rabbinic Jewish origin" and was most likely produced in Edessa, then the cultural center of the Syriac-speaking world, between the first and third centuries AD (Weitzman). It is interesting that studies have shown that Edessa was a city with a more sizeable Christian population than most Mesopotamian cities, while having a smaller Jewish presence (Russell, "Nisibis"). This allows for the possibility that the "Jewish" version of the Old Testament text used by Christians was even more closely connected with their multi-hued background than it might otherwise have been, since even the Jews in the region were affected by the same influences felt by the Christians. The fact that books were hand copied as well as the natural isolation of groups from each other due to distance or political upheavals has meant that the biblical canon has been more fluid among Syrian Christians than the canons of the western church (Brock, *Bible*).

How did the Syrians read their Bibles? There was a difference between their cultural milieu and that of the Roman world. Jewish methods and interpretation were better known among the Syrians than among their western counterparts. The shared Aramaic language allowed Syrian Christians to make direct use of Jewish sources. The different array of theological problems and challenges thrown up by having different opponents for religious debate also had an important impact. So, for example, Ephraem the Syrian's treatment of the six days of creation in his commentary on Genesis was intended as an argument against the teachings of Bar Daisan, a native philosopher of Edessa. There was more than just a desire to argue theology with opponents in the Christian use of Scripture, however; Syrian Christians were determined miners of the Bible for spiritual truth. It is in this realm that they have the most interest for Christians of the twenty-first century. Sebastian Brock, the preeminent scholar of Syriac matters at the present time, explains clearly that

> The Syriac fathers are interested both in "factual," or "historical," and in "spiritual" interpretation, though not surprisingly they pay greater attention to the latter. Since modern historical understanding of the Bible and its background is vastly superior to that of the Syriac Fathers (thanks to the advances in biblical scholarship over the last century), what the Syriac Fathers have to say on the level of historical interpretation is very rarely of more than antiquarian interest. What they have to say in the area of spiritual interpretation, however, has by no means been superseded, and much of what they say can be just as meaningful today as it was to their own times. (Brock, *Bible*, p. 55)

This searching for spiritual meaning took place in a world that, according to their understanding, was filled with things that could link human beings to God. They thought of the search for knowledge of God and His purposes that focused on the Bible as the investigation of only part of God's self-revelation to, and communication with, His creation. This is not evidence of an idea that creatures have a natural ability to know God, but rather of a conviction that God is so merciful and loving that He reveals Himself to them as a matter of course. As St. Ephraem the Syrian says in one of his hymns:

> My smallness has spoken about you because Your Greatness was willing
>
> To fall into the realm of words and be in the realm of speech
>
> So that You could be an aid to speech and hearing.
> (Russell, "Scripture," 174)

Thus, this expansive view of the knowledge of God that humans can hope to attain is accompanied by a lively sense of God's complete transcendence of the created realm. Because Scripture is a focused, *explicit* revelation by God to human beings, it is much more important than the less comprehended revelations that surround us all the time. We can only understand this way of thinking of the connection between God and the world if we realize that it is intended to express both His overwhelming mercy and the endless gulf that He must pass over to reach His creatures (Koonammakkal, all works).

With that idea in mind, we can pass to a consideration of how the Syrians understood the Psalms. We must remember, however, that not only did they think of the Psalms as part of the revelation found in Scripture, but they thought of the Bible as the central part of God's larger reaching out to His creation with the intention of drawing it near to Him and making it what He had always intended it to be. God's actions are always undertaken with salvation in mind in the Syrian Christian imagination, and we can only grasp their treatment of the Psalms if we keep that larger context at the front of our thoughts.

To understand Syrian commentaries on Psalm 29 it is necessary to begin with Theodore of Mopsuestia (350?–428) for to many Syrian Christians he remained "the interpreter" of the Bible. His commentary on the book of Psalms is only partially extant and highly dependent on his teacher, Diodore of Tarsus. This was one of Theodore's first ventures into scriptural interpretation, but it bears the distinctive characteristics of his mature works: setting the texts in events of Old Testament narratives, use of Greek, Hebrew and Syriac textual traditions (his knowledge of Hebrew and Syriac was definitely not fluent), arguments made from Greek translations of the Bible; and conviction of the divine inspiration of all passages. With other members of the Antiochene school of biblical interpretation, Theodore insisted on taking the biblical text literally; however, the book of Psalms contains poetic works that necessitated poetic interpretation and Theodore was willing to recognize metaphor and allegory; still the meaning needed to conform to the world of ancient Judah and Israel. It should be kept in mind that this was the work of a very young man (some say he began it at the age of 18) and one not yet comfortable with the religious life.

Psalm 29 (for Theodore: Psalm 28) is taken as a prophetic psalm by David sung in the very voice of King Hezekiah of Judah. The historical background for the poem is understood as the Assyrian invasion of Judah, siege of Jerusalem, and miraculous departure of the Assyrian army (2 Kgs 19). Indeed this psalm of David is understood by Theodore to reflect the late period of Hezekiah's life when he repents of not having properly given thanks to God for saving Jerusalem; it is then an admonition by God to all those who come later never to forget to thank God for events that turn out well. Actual commentary on the text is sparsely preserved as a series of notes. The cedars of Lebanon in verse 5 are taken to be a reference to the invading Assyrian army, for they were mighty. In verse 6 Theodore insists [incorrectly] that translations that read "calf" are in error, and the term is actually to be understood as referring to slender, weak plants in oppositional parallel to the cedars of the previous lines. Thus, God defeats the Assyrians as though they were mere trifles rather than a mighty host. He also translates "make skip" as "beats into a powder," so the defeat of the Assyrians is complete. "Sirion" is understood by Theodore to refer to the "beloved" by which he understands "Israel," and with the Septuagint, reads the last animal of verse 6 as "unicorn." His interpretation of verse 8 is novel: the wilderness refers to the land which the Assyrians have laid waste, hence "wilderness," while the voice of the Lord will shake it as in creating an earthquake there. "Kadesh" he reads as the similar Hebrew word *qodesh*, "holy," and so understands that the land saved from the Assyrian horde was literally the Holy Land. His interpretation underlies the great Syrian commentaries.

Syrian Christians and the Psalms

The destruction of the legacy of the Syrian Christians is particularly grievous when it comes to their biblical commentaries. These works often tended to be extremely lengthy and so were liable to being copied only in excerpts. They also tended to be cited and referred to by other authors who cited passages rather than copied complete works. The Psalter, which tended to inspire the production of very full treatments because of its prominence in Christian worship especially among those living lives dedicated to prayer and mediation, found its commentaries disappearing at a great rate. It is worthwhile setting out a list of works that survived into the modern age:

Daniel of Ṣalah Commentary on the Psalms	(fl. mid 6th cent.)	(Syrian Orthodox)
Ishodad of Merv	Commentary on the Bible (fl. mid 9th cent.)	(Church of the East)
Moshe Bar Kepha	Commentary on the Old Testament (+903)	(Syrian Orthodox)
Dionysius Bar Salibi	Commentary on the Old Testament (+1171)	(Syrian Orthodox)
Gregory Bar Hebraeus	*Treasure of Mysteries* (+1286)	(Syrian Orthodox)

These are the main materials that are left, though there are some others. None of these is available in easy-to-find editions in a modern western language, though David Taylor of Oxford University is preparing an edition with translation of the complete commentary of Daniel of Ṣalah, which will facilitate English access to a major stream of Syrian Christian biblical exegesis.

The commentary of Daniel Ṣalah was begun in 541 or 542. Unfortunately, the portion of the commentary that treats Psalm 29 is not available, so we cannot examine it in detail. However, it is worth taking a moment to see how Daniel orients himself toward the Psalter in general, as he is our earliest surviving voice from Syrian traditions. His guiding assumptions are ones that fit into the main stream of early Christian interpretation of the Psalms in the eastern Mediterranean. He assumes that the whole Psalter stems from David. So, for example, he reads Psalm 8 as expressing David's joy at the moving of the Ark of the Covenant from Philistia to Jerusalem (2 Samuel 6). He assumes that the Psalter is "consonant with the rest of scripture," as Cowe expresses it. He thinks that the psalms are not placed in random order but that their meaning can be revealed by an attention to the collection as a whole. As such, the last fifty psalms can be read as an ascent to spiritual awareness and can aid the reader in that ascent. Cowe finds a quite regular order in how Daniel treats the psalms: general theme, historical setting, sermonic unfolding of the moral, and a closing prayer. This format is one of Cowe's chief reasons for suggesting that a desire to aid the living of a monastic life lay behind the writing of the commentary and also informs his suggestion that they were intended for communal reading. The standard form would make them easier to follow for the listeners.

There are two things that leap out at us as we read this description. The first is that this "historical" approach to reading the Psalms is not, in fact, historical at all, according to our use of that word. The second is Daniel's desire to find sustenance for the living out of the Christian vocation in Scripture. Daniel's work supports O'Keefe's potent argument that we misunderstand ancient interpretation if we think that Antiochene writers were "more historical" than Alexandrians (O'Keefe). The second point is more general and more important: Daniel of Ṣalah's approach lives in the heart of the church because it is one that seeks to ground the reader (or listener) in the Bible as he struggles in the world. This pastoral reading of Scripture and of the Psalms goes back as far as we can trace it and Daniel of Ṣalah's work shows that the earliest Syrian author we have was firmly in that tradition of practical, religious application of the Psalms to the believer's religious life.

Ishodad of Merv wrote commentaries on the whole of the Christian Bible. These made use of different Greek translations of the Old Testament (Aquila, Septuagint, Symmachus, and Theodotion) as well as the Peshitta. His breadth of sources used for the test of the Psalter was itself beyond the power, or imagination, of most western writers of his time. His work, as one might expect with a project of such size, is more a set of notes on selected verses in the Psalms than a line-by-line commentary on the whole Psalter.

A particularly interesting section of his work is the Introduction to the Old Testament. Ishodad sets out there some of his general ideas of what the study of Scripture ought to entail and what the Bible really is. He begins by discussing the Septuagint, Aquila, Symmachus, Theodotion, and Origen's *Hexapla* before he progresses to versions in his own language. He describes the different types of literature contained in the Old Testament and examines what can be known or surmised about the education received by Moses and Solomon (as being two prominent authors of scriptural books). This was an approach and range of subjects that shows a scholarly sensibility along the lines of modern biblical research.

Ishodad shows great respect for the writing and judgment of Theodore of Mopsuestia, as one would expect in a scholar of the Church of the East. Since Theodore thought that most of the psalms sprang from known events in the history of Israel, he strove to link them with what he thought were their proper circumstances. In Ishodad's opinion, in accord with Theodore, the proper historical background of Psalm 29 was the period of Hezekiah and the life of Israel at that time (2 Kgs 16:20—20:21; Isa 36-39; 2 Chr 29-32).

One of the results of the approach which Ishodad followed was that the psalms were pulled into the public life of Israel, as opposed to their being thought of as having sprung from private religious life or worship. This would tend to remove the psalms from practical application in the primary instance; it is true that Antiochene writers applied psalms to the religious lives of Christians, but must it not have had a different flavor for them if they thought that the religious use was not a part of their natural place in history?

Ishodad, in the tradition of Theodore of Mopsuestia, provides nine main comments on Psalm 29. They all key on making clear how the historical background of the reign of Hezekiah and the waning days of the divided kingdoms of Judah and Israel are expressed in the psalm's imagery. According to Ishodad, the "mighty ones" of verse 1 are the Jews, so called because of their closeness to God. The "waters" of verse 3 are the Assyrians because of their great numbers and their washing forward to sweep away the kingdoms. The "flashes of lightning" (NIV) or "fiery flame" (NAB: this is the reading Ishodad follows) in verse 7 are also the Assyrians because of their devouring nature. Lest this psalm seem to raise the Assyrians over God's chosen people, Ishodad points out that the "cedars" of verse 5, which the Lord breaks, are also the Assyrians, because of their lofty pride. The sum is a picture in which the sovereignty of God over the world is emphasized and the description in the psalm of what might appear as "acts of nature" are referred to God directly as evidence of his on-going involvement in the events of the world.

Moshe Bar Kepha produced an "Introduction to the Psalms of David." This is a particularly useful work for us, since it addresses the sort of questions that allow us to look inside the mind of a thoughtful Christian of a very different era to see how he thought about the Psalter and how he imagined it against the backdrop of the whole scriptural canon. Almost the first sentence in his work reads:

> Each of the holy books has a particular purpose and teaches on one or two subjects, more or less. This book of Psalms unites

in itself the purposes of all the Prophets and on all the subjects about which they teach it teaches eloquently.

Moshe subscribes to the common Christian idea that the psalms treat of everything that relates to religious life and all areas of religious truth. They teach all the virtues, including "not to be afraid when one is derided by one's adversaries." They teach us all the mysteries of the Messiah; that is to say, Moshe supports Christological readings of some of the psalms. He held to the uniqueness in Scripture of David's use of music to accompany his oracles. He declared that God mixed attractive melodies with his laws and ordinances as a doctor mixes honey with bitter medicine; an idea which also appears in Bar Hebraeus' introduction to his work as a quotation from Basil of Caesarea. Moshe also found the division of the Psalter into three sets of fifty psalms meaningful demonstrating that he used a Psalter of 150 psalms unlike many Syrian Christians whose book of Psalms include Psalm 151. He says: "By the three 50s we praise the Three Holy Persons, the Father, the Son and the Holy Spirit, Who are the one true God. In the same way, by the three 50s, we praise and confess the Christ Who has delivered us from three enemies: Satan, sin and death." He carries on with more ruminations on the meaning of the number 50, but the above is enough to show that Moshe thought that the arrangement and size of the Psalter instructed the reader, just as the contents does.

The last thing for us to note is that Père Vosté mentions that in chapter 23 of his introduction Moshe discusses the differences that appear when the Hebrew, Greek and Syriac numeration and division of the verses of the psalms are compared. This shows that he had access to these different versions to study and was able to consider the Psalms both as they sat on the page before him in the translation that he used for his own worship as well as in their other garbs in other languages. This does not seem to have interfered with his religious use of them but rather appears to have provided him with another lens through which to view this text around which his own worship was centered. His scholarship did not war against his devotion.

Dionysius Bar Salibi is an extremely interesting figure to consider. His methodical mind applied itself to the task of trying to grasp the Scripture in all its richness and multi-layered quality and came up with a novel, and demanding, approach to piercing through the veil between the believer and God's revelation. As Ryan says in his introduction:

> What is unique about Bar Salibi's *Commentary on the Old Testament* is that it contains two separate commentaries, one factual, and another that is described variously as spiritual, spiritual and factual, or mixed, for most books of the Old Testament. It is this bifurcation of the material, the separation into two or three columns, presented in most manuscripts in synoptic fashion, that is distinctive.

That picture of a two or three columned commentary on a single passage or psalm is worth pondering. That arrangement of material allows the reader more than one approach to the psalm. The reader could read through one column of the commentary and consider the psalm on only one level. The reader could try to read the commentaries before turning to the psalm and then have their comments in mind as he looked at the text itself. I am convinced that this flexibility of use was one of Bar Salibi's main motives in producing such a large work. He was not only recognizing, but was trying to spur on, the reader's multi-valent interaction with Scripture. He must have wanted to encourage each reader of his work to reflect on the scriptural text in a number of different ways, especially in different readings of his work, and so to come to a deeper and more nuanced relationship with what God was revealing to him in those words. This sort of work must have sprung from a conviction of the Bible's character as a living text, since only so could this variety have been helpful rather than misleading. Bar Salibi showed a very high understanding of Scripture as a means of reaching God as well as great faith in the willingness and ability of his audience to grapple with the Bible to their profit, rather than to their confusion.

Bar Salibi made use of Hebrew, Greek and Peshitta versions of the text. He knew of more than one Greek version, but did not make frequent use of them for comparative purposes. Ryan is convinced that his primary audience was monastic, so it may be thought these scholarly details were only useful to a certain degree for his readers. We do not have his treatment of Psalm 29, so we can only note these generalities: a deep appreciation for the sacred nature of the text, a scholarly awareness of the variety of the text in different languages, and in different versions in the same language and confidence in the seriousness of the purpose and intelligence of his audience. Those suffice to provide us with a sense of the man and his work.

Gregory Bar Habraeus brings us to one of the great personages of Syrian Christianity. Maphrian (the second ranking cleric) of the Syrian Orthodox Church, scholar, ecumenist, medical doctor, historian, writer of theological and devotional works, Bar Hebraeus was an astounding figure in the opinion of his contemporaries. He was a prolific writer, but few of his works are easily available. His work on the psalms is called "Scholia" because they are a series of disconnected notes on particular points rather than a connected commentary on the whole text of the Psalter, but they give a sense of him as a scholar and student of the Psalms.

Bar Hebraeus was a scholar and had a scholar's instincts. When he cited earlier writers he cited them by name to keep things clear for himself and for his reader. The list of those he cites in the introduction to his *Scholia on the Psalms* is interesting because it demonstrates the breadth of his reading and of his view of the church: Athanasius, Hippolytus, Basil, Origen, Epipanius, and Daniel of Ṣalah. This stretches geographically from Rome to Egypt and intellectually from Alexandria to Cappadocia. That is quite an expansive reach and shows how well connected to the rest of the church a Christian scholar could be in Persia of the thirteenth century. He has chosen selections from these authors in which they discuss the history of the collection of the psalms and uses them to discuss the history of the Psalter in Jewish circles before the fixing of the Old Testament text. These show that he had a sense of the history of books and texts that was separate from their theological and religious value. Gregory Bar Hebraeus did not feel his faith in the inspiration of the Psalter was challenged by having a clear idea of the variety of detail in or the history of ancient books.

What does Bar Hebraeus say of Psalm 29? With almost all early Jews and Christians he holds, with the psalm's heading, that it is the work of David, but, in accord with Theodore of Mopsuestia, written "in the person of Hezekiah in gratitude for deliverance from the Assyrians. A sacrificial intention of the psalm is understood, both as thanksgiving and with the reference to the "young rams" for sacrifice found only in the Greek (v. 1). With a Greek addition to the heading of the psalm and in accord with Talmud (*Sukkah*), he places the proper time for reciting the psalm at the Feast of Booths; he then cites Athanasius as reading this as the going out of the Jews and the coming in of the gentiles. Making these constant references to the textual variants in the different language texts of the psalm (including Armenian and the various Greek versions from the Jews) he works his way through the psalm, mostly along the lines set out by Daniel of Ṣalah in the wake of the Antiochene Greeks before him. His passages, which are daunting in their density at first reading, cite scholars, translations, and debates over meaning in condensed comments. In an age in which books were few and expensive, he provided the readers with the advantage that a large selection of scarce but relevant works would have had: a selection of other readings that seem possible and interesting. These notes correspond to what a modern scholarly translation of the Bible provides in its footnotes.

Bar Hebraeus believed that the images in the psalm refer to the world and time of Hezekiah and makes those connections, but he also makes room for those who wish to read the Psalm as having universal spiritual lessons to teach to all who read it. This is the purpose of his connection between the "flood" of verse 11 and "the multitude of the believers" that he mentions in his scholia. The "waters" of verse 3, and the cedars of verse 5 are both seen as references to the Assyrians, but Bar Hebraeus allows for the possibility that the "voice of the Lord" over the waters also refers to the voice of the Father at the Jordan River (Jesus' Baptism). He provides two readings of verse 6: either it reads "make them skip like calves," in which case it means the joy of the Jews on the destruction of the Assyrians, or it reads "beat them like calves," in which case it refers to the Assyrians being destroyed by God and to the latter he adds Theodore's "puny plants" interpretation. He equates the "unicorn" of verse six with the hard-to-capture mountain animal rimah that he says has but one horn. Verse 7 represents God taking away the Assyrians from the ten tribes of Israel with the fire being the Assyrians. In verse 8 Jerusalem as the holy city makes the area where the Assyrians encamped "holy" (the Theodorian translation of Kadesh). and verse 9 is taken as the uprooting of trees and with the phrase "strengthens the hinds/female of the stags" (the problem of translating this term is laid out) again a double option is provided: either it is the Assyrians who are the hinds removed by God, or it is the Israelites who are hinds empowered to remove the Assyrians. In the end, God turns back the violence ("flood") and reigns in Jerusalem forever. Perhaps this is a suitable place to end our visit to the ancient Near East.

Syrian Christians read the Psalms as a part of their daily prayers, as was universal early Christian practice. They showed a real desire to use their knowledge of the various language and text traditions of the Bible to understand it better and to see it more clearly and they did not want to lose the spiritual meaning because of their search for the historical background, Bar Salibi going so far as to write a double (or triple) commentary on the Psalter in order to preserve its multiple meanings. They saw the Psalter as an outgrowth of the life of Israel and that conviction carries with it a picture of the Bible as a record of God's dealings with his people in the world as well as a living thing with real and present spiritual force. They can find God in it speaking to them so that they can be part of the larger church beyond their homeland by incorporating their wisdom in their devotional study of Scripture.

Bar Hebraeus died in Persia when it was ruled by the Mongol successors of Ghengis Khan but his imagination carried him throughout the Christian world, and beyond, in his search for knowledge and wisdom. In that, at least, he was a representative of the best instincts of his own tradition and serves as a challenge to those who do not ever think to look backwards in time or eastwards in direction to find their Christian brothers and sisters who loved the Lord and sought for Him with their whole hearts.

Bibliography

Baumer, Christoph. *The Church of the East: An Illustrated History of Assyrian Christianity.* New York: I. B. Tauris, 2006.

Becker, Adam H. *Fear of God and the Beginning of Wisdom: The School of Nisibis and the Development of Scholastic Culture in Late Antique Mesopotamia.* Philadelphia: University of Pennsylvania Press, 2006.

Brock, Sebastian P. *The Bible in the Syriac Tradition.* Kerala, India: St. Ephrem Ecumenical Research Institute, 1988.

———. *A Brief Outline of Syriac Literature.* Moran Etho 9. Kottayam, India: St. Ephrem Ecumenical Research Institute, 1997.

———. *An Introduction to Syriac Studies.* Rev. 2nd ed. Piscatawaqay, NJ: Gorgias, 2006.

———. *The Luminous Eye: The Spiritual World View of Saint Ephrem the Syrian.* Kalamazoo, Mich.: Cistercian, 1992.

Chapin, Richard Steven. "Mesopotamian Scholasticism: A Comparison of the Jewish and Christian 'Schools.'" Ph.D. diss., Hebrew Union College—Jewish Institute of Religion, 1990.

Cowe, S. Peter. "Daniel of Ṣalah as Commentator on the Psalter." *Studia Patristica* 20 (1989) 152–59.

Diodore of Tarsus. *Commentary on Psalms 1–51*. Translated with a commentary by Robert C. Hill. Writings from the Greco-Roman World 9. Atlanta: Society of Biblical Literature, 2005.

Drijvers, H. J. W. *Cults and Beliefs at Edessa*. Leiden: Brill, 1980.

Ephraem the Syrian. *St. Ephrem the Syrian Selected Prose Works*. Translated by Edward G. Matthews, Jr., and Joseph P Amar. FC 91. Washington, DC: Catholic University of America, 1994.

Froehlich, Karlfried, editor. *Biblical Interpretation in the Early Church*. Philadelphia: Fortress, 1984.

Gilman, Ian, and Hans-Joachim Klimkeit, *Christians in Asia before 1500*. Ann Arbor: University of Michigan Press, 1999.

Griffith, Sidney H. *"Faith Adoring the Mystery": Reading the Bible with St. Ephraem the Syrian*. Milwaukee: Marquette University Press, 1997.

Išoʻdad of Merv. *Commentaire de Išoʻdad of Merv sur l'Ancien Testament. VI: Psaumes*. Edited by Ceslas van den Eynde. CSCO 433–34. Scriptores Syri 185. Louvain: Peeters, 1981.

Koonammakkal, Thomas. "Ephrem's Idea of Revelation as Divine Pedagogy." *The Harp* 16 (2003) 355–64.

———. "Ephrem's Imagery of Chasm." In *Symposium Syriacum VII*. OrChrAn 256. 175–83. Rome: Pontificio Istituto Orientale, 1998.

———. "The Self-Revealing God and Man in Ephrem." *The Harp* 6 (1993) 233–48.

LaGarde, Paul de. *Praetermissorum Libri Duo*. Göttingen: Dieterich, 1879.

Moffett, Samuel Hugh. *A History of Christianity in Asia. Volume 1: Beginnings to 1500*. 2nd rev. ed. Maryknoll, NY: Orbis Books, 1998.

O'Keefe, John J. "'A Letter that Killeth': Toward a reassessment of Antiochene Exegesis, or Diodore, Theodore and Theodoret on the Psalms." *JECS* 8 (2000) 83–104.

———, and R. R. Reno. *Sanctified Vision: An Introduction to Early Christian Interpretation of the Bible*. Baltimore: Johns Hopkins University Press, 2005.

Ortiz de Urbina, Ignatius. *Patrologia Syriaca*. 2nd ed. Rome: Pontificium Institutum Orientalium Studiorum, 1965.

Ross, Steven K. *Roman Edessa: Politics and Culture on the Eastern Fringes of the Roman Empire, 114–242 CE*. London: Routledge, 2001.

Rubenstein, Jeffrey L. *The Culture of the Babylonian Talmud*. Baltimore: Johns Hopkins University Press, 2003.

Russell, Paul S. "Making Sense of Scripture: An Early Attempt by St. Ephraem the Syrian." *Comm* 28 (2001) 171–201.

———. "Nisibis as the Background to the Life and Work of Ephraem the Syrian." *Hugoye* 8 (2005).

Ryan, Stephen Desmond. "Studies in Bar Salibi's Commentary on the Psalms." PhD dissertation, Harvard University, 2001.

Siegel, Julius L. "The Scholia of Bar Hebraeus on the Book of the Psalms." PhD dissertation, University of Chicago, 1928.

Taylor, David G. K. "The Manuscript Tradition of Daniel of Ṣalaḥ's Psalm Commentary." In *Symposium Syriacum VII*. OrChrAn 256. 61–69. Rome: Pontificio Istituto Orientale, 1998.

Theodore of Mopsuestia. *Commentary on Psalms 1–81*. Translated by Robert C. Hill. WGRW 5. Atlanta: Society of Biblical Literature, 2006.

Vosté, J. M. "L'Introduction de Mar Išoʻdad de Merw (c. 850) aux Livres de L'Ancien Testament." *Bib* 26 (1945) 182–202.

———. "L'Introduction de Moshe Bar Kepha aux Psaumes de David." *RB* 38 (1929) 214–28.

Weitzman, Michael P. *The Syriac Version of the Old Testament: An Introduction.* Cambridge: Cambridge University Press, 1999.

6

Not Elijah's God

Medieval Jewish and Christian Interpretation of Psalm 29

Stacy Davis

ANY HISTORY OF INTERPRETATION STUDY, SUCH AS THIS CHAPTER ON medieval Jewish and Christian interpretation of Psalm 29, may easily become a doorstop instead of a pamphlet. Numerous exegetes and their twists and turns can render an analysis serpentine at best, which is why the editor wisely assigned reasonable page limits for the wellbeing of author and reader alike. Consequently, the next several pages will function as an appetizer to the banquet that is medieval Jewish and Christian commentary, offering a taste of its delights and hopefully whetting the palate for further study. Interpretation of Psalm 29:3–9 and its characterization of "the voice of the Lord" exemplifies the hermeneutical presuppositions of the time. Specifically, both religious traditions argued for multiple senses of Scripture and the importance of intertextuality, or using one biblical text to explain another. Also, both traditions read the psalm of praise as a praise of God's loud voice, in contrast to the "voice of a small whisper" [*qol demamah daqah*] that Elijah hears in 1 Kings 19:5. The Lord's bellowing is basic dough within which exegetes from both faiths added ingredients of God's saving acts, past and present. The figure of Jesus, however, gave medieval Christian exegesis a distinctive and occasionally anti-Jewish texture, as we will see.

Medieval Jewish interpreters built upon the foundation laid by their rabbinic predecessors. Rabbinic hermeneutics emphasized intertextuality and different ways to read Scripture. Specifically, exegetes could use *peshat*, the interpretation of a verse or verses within their immediate biblical context, and *derash*, a less literal and more homiletical approach. Medieval Jewish scholars adapted *peshat* and *derash*; *peshat* becomes the plain meaning of the Hebrew words, in contrast to the spiritual interpretations characteristic of *derash*. *Peshat* and *derash* eventually make up half of the acronym PaRDes, the Jewish fourfold sense of Scripture, with *remez* being the moral sense and *sod* the mystical sense. During medieval times Jewish exegesis focused upon *peshat*, but this focus did not stifle the creativity for which rabbinic *derash* was noteworthy. In the case of Psalm 29 its classification as *aggadah* (a non-legal text) and not *halakhah* (a text from which a legal commandment derives) may help to explain the exegetical diversity found among Rashi, Rashbam, and David Kimchi.

Similar to their Jewish counterparts, medieval Christian interpreters also had a fourfold sense of Scripture, an expansion of the distinction between the letter and the spirit first articulated by Paul in Galatians 4:21–31 and 2 Corinthians 3:6, and later by Origen. The literal sense analyzes a text's historical context and serves as the foundation for the three spiritual senses: allegory (the Christological sense), tropology (the moral/ethical sense) and anagogy (the eschatological/end-of-time sense). Although the literal sense became more popular during the medieval period, the Christian belief in the authority of Scripture and tradition meant that the older readings of biblical texts maintained their value. Patristic exegetes, such as Augustine, were copied by interpreters hundreds of years later and presented without explanation as definitive readings of the text. Particularly with the Psalms, a primary biblical source of doctrine for medieval Christians, the literal sense's popularity rarely appeared. The two main advocates of the literal sense, Hugh and Andrew of St. Victor, who did not comment on the Psalms, slanted their interpretations of the Bible towards the literal sense. With the notable exception of Nicholas of Lyra, a fourteenth-century Franciscan who focused upon the literal sense and studied Jewish exegesis as well as Christian traditional commentaries, Christian interpretation of Psalm 29 expanded the earlier patristic reading. Also, the principle of intertextuality thrived in the form of prooftexting, or using one verse or a series of verses to "prove" the truth of another biblical passage or strengthen a theological claim. It is now time to see how the medieval exegetes remained faithful to these hermeneutical traditions.

Rabbi Solomon ben Isaac of Troyes, or Rashi (1040–1106) is the most famous of the medieval Jewish biblical scholars. Indeed, the first Hebrew book to come off a printing press, in 1475, was Rashi's Torah Commentary, printed seven years before the Hebrew Bible itself (Marcus, 412; Pearl, 94). For Psalm 29 Rashi connected God's voice to God's having given the Torah to Israel and God's dominion over other nations. God's powerful voice converses with Moses in Exodus 19:19 and prepares to give him the commandments. The voice of God that breaks trees in Psalm 29:5 also breaks foreign nations such as Assyria, in accord with Isaiah 30:31: "The Assyrian will be terror-stricken at the voice of the Lord." The trees go out to hear the Torah being given to Israel and they respond by skipping (Psalm 29:6). God's voice splits flames of fire that write on the stone tablets. Rashi quoted the beginning of Deuteronomy 5:26 ("For who is there of all flesh . . .") to emphasize the overwhelming might of this voice; the rest of the verse concludes as follows: "that has heard the voice of the living God speaking out of fire, as we have, and remained alive?" The wilderness of Kadesh refers to Sinai where Israel received the Torah and its distinctive identity. Just as God's voice strips trees, it also destroys nations like the Amorites, "whose height was like the height of cedars" (Amos 2:9). Rashi's use of biblical texts from the Torah (Exodus, Deuteronomy) and the prophets (Isaiah, Amos) established that Psalm 29 emphasizes God as Israel's God.

Rashi's grandson, Samuel ben Meir, or Rashbam (1083—1174) continued his grandfather's biblically-based approach, but with a shift in emphasis. Rashbam connected God's voice to the creation narrative in Genesis 1. "The voice of the Lord breaks the cedars" (Psalm 29:5) was understood to have taken place on the third day of creation when God formed plants and trees (Gen 1:11–13); the intial breaking enables the trees to become perfect. The "flames of fire," of verse 7, hint at the fourth day of creation when the sun, moon and stars came into being (Gen 1:14–19). God's presence in the wilderness (Ps 29:8) refers to the fifth day of creation when all birds appear (Gen 1:20–23). Notably, Rashbam's exegesis of Psalm 29:9a introduced a textual ambiguity that reappeared throughout the medieval period. *Qol YHWH yaḥolel 'ayyalot* may be translated in two ways because the phrase *yaḥolel 'ayyalot* can be read either as "causes the oaks to whirl" or "causes the deer to calve." The Latin translation, *praeparantis cervos*, follows the second option, but the Hebrew exegetes could take either option, or, in the case of David

Kimchi, both options. Kimchi's first reading of Psalm 29:9a argued that God's voice facilitates conception, but his second reading claimed that the writhing deer are mighty rulers, described earlier as cedars and mountains, and that falling trees will strip forests bare. Rashbam chose to continue his creation comparison by utilizing the second option; the deer giving birth refer to their day of creation, the sixth day (Gen 1:24–26). Rashbam's exegesis maintained Rashi's emphasis upon the power of God's voice, but the power generates life instead of destroying it and therefore is less intimidating.

David Kimchi (1160–1235) echoed the exegesis of his predecessors. God's frightening voice gives the Torah to Israel; according to *peshat*, however, the psalm praises God's creation. Kimchi wrote, "And the commentators explain the psalm in the plain sense [literally *derekh peshato*, or "the way of its *peshat*"] concerning the wonders of creation, the sights in the earth" (Kimchi, 69). He continued by citing rabbi Abraham ben Ezra (1089/92—1164/67) who had explained the heavenly beings in Psalm 29:1 as being the stars which protect the temple court. Building on this Kimchi stated that God's voice in Psalm 29:3 brings rain, as Job 5:9–10 states, as well as lightning and hail which break the cedars in Psalm 29:5.

Most distinctively, Kimchi offered a third interpretation of the voice of the Lord: "but therefore in my opinion, this psalm [is] in preparation of the days of the messiah" (Kimchi, 70). The head king rules over the other kings, the cedars that break (Ps 29:5), like Assyria (Ezek 31:3), and the mountains that he makes disappear (Isa 54:10). The messiah also will wipe out the sea according to Jeremiah 51:36 and Isaiah 11:15, which is alluded to in Psalm 29:3. The primary indication that Kimchi was interpreting messianically was his use of Ezekiel 38:22 to explain the description of God's voice as powerful and majestic in Psalm 29:4. Ezekiel 38–39 is an apocalyptic narrative describing the final defeat of Gog and Magog culminating in Israel's return to its own land. Kimchi's final comment on the psalm reads: God will "bless his people with peace [Ps 29:11] because in the future there will be no war against them" (Kimchi, 71).

Kimchi's interpretation of Psalm 29 as messianic was original, but his approach was not. His reference to *peshat* aside, he, Rashi and Rashbam utilized the psalm to preach about God's glory, either in past acts of creation and covenant making or future messianic deeds. The psalm's literal words precipitated homiletical discourse about their possible deeper meanings. A similar pattern appeared in medieval Christian exegesis.

The *Glossa Ordinaria*, developed under the direction of Anselm (1033–1109), became the standard textbook for medieval Christian exegetical study; in essence it generally restated the insights of earlier commentators. The *Glossa* built upon Cassian's (360?–435) argument that God's voice is Christ's preaching, as well as Gregory the Great's (540–604) claim that God turns "a spirit of fear into a spirit of wisdom" (p. 486). Isaiah 11:2–3, read messianically by Christians in the Latin Vulgate, argues that God gives Jesus the favored one "a spirit of wisdom and understanding, a spirit of counsel and strength, a spirit of knowledge and piety, and the spirit of the fear of the Lord will fill him." God's voice breaks the cedars of Lebanon, or all proud Jews and Gentiles. Just as a cedar tree becomes valuable only if cut down, a sinner gains utility only after being humbled, a necessary prerequisite for conversion to the way of Christ. The Vulgate's translation of Psalm 29:6b, reads instead of "and Sirion like a young wild ox": "loves [them] just as the child of the unicorn." In interpreting this text Christ was the beloved child of the unicorn, a descendant of the Jewish people who take pride in the Torah; he also died as a Jew. This brief historical Jesus moment, however, is interrupted by the *Glossa*'s observation that the desert of Kadesh, shattered by God's voice in verse 8, is the disobedient, specifically "the Jews, who do not have the sanctity of the law, that is spiritual understanding." According to Jerome (342?–420), interpreting Scripture anagogically was the highest form of understanding, and Augustine (354–430) concludes that only through conversion to Christianity will Jews cease to be a desert. For the *Glossa*, reading the First Testament christologically also meant reading comabatively in anti-Jewish terms. It remains to be seen whether such reading was the consequence of utilizing patristic commentary or was a contemporary charactersitic of medieval Christian exegesis.

Bruno di Segni (1045?–1123) took a similar approach as did the *Glossa*. God's voice equals preaching, but the preaching occurs "when holy preachers preach God's word in the church through the inspiration of the Holy Spirit" (p. 787). Through the ministers God's voice facilitates baptism, which brings about miracles in the physical and spiritual worlds (Psalm 29:4). According to Bruno, God's voice humiliates the cedars (v. 5) which are "the rich and powerful of this age" (Bruno di Segni,

788); some cedars will convert, but according to Matthew 3:10, others will end up in hell. The cedars of Lebanon, however, are Jerusalem and its citizens, destroyed by God with the fall of the Second Temple in 70 CE, as Zechariah 11:1 predicted. Regarding Psalm 29:6, the sacrifices mandated in the Torah bore no fruit, but the sacrificial animals were destroyed just like the cedars. In contrast, Matthew 12:18 was cited as proof that Christ is the living and beloved unicorn, but the unicorn also could be the church by citing the Song of Solomon 5:10 and 8:14. Bruno, however, favors the first interpretation because of 1 Samuel 2:10, a praise of an earthly ruler that Bruno reads messianically: "The Lord will judge the ends of the earth; he will give strength to his king, and exalt the power of his anointed" [Vulgate: *et sublimavit cornu* christi *sui*]. The physical upheaval described in verses 7–8, with God's voice spewing fire and shaking deserts, refers to the conflict between Jewish and Gentile Christians, which Peter resolved in favor of the Gentile Chrisitans (Acts 10–11). Bruno argues that God intends to save both groups because John the Baptist preaches to Jews in Luke 3:11 and soldiers (presumably Roman) in Luke 3:14.

Bruno returned to his original claim that God's voice is ecclesial preaching in his analysis of Psalm 29:9. "Who are the deer if we do not recognize the apostles, agile in running, quick in preaching, killing serpents, not fearing magic and desirous of the fountains of water [a likely reference to baptismal fonts]? The Lord, however, prepares them to preach the Gospel, and to reveal and explain the scriptures" (Bruno di Segni, 789). Bruno's proof was Revelation 5:5, where the apostle John is found worthy to see the scroll and its seals opened. As a bishop and later an abbot, Bruno sees himself in that apostolic line, with its attendant rights and privileges, and for him, emphasizing apostolic succession and power proves to be more important than anti-Jewish interpretation.

For Peter Lombard (1100–1160) glossing Psalm 29 meant being faithful to the observations of earlier exegetes, especially Cassian, and repeating the *Glossa*. Consequently, little original material may be found in his commentary. Lombard did argue, however, that Christ's preaching ("the voice of the Lord") brings down the conversion power of the Holy Spirit. Notably, Lombard downplays the *Glossa*'s anti-Jewish rhetoric in two places. First, God's voice does break the Jewish people ("cedars of Lebanon"), but Lombard suggests that salvation will belong to some of them at the end of time. Second, the desert of Kadesh is not the Jewish people, but "according to the letter is the place where water was given from the rock" in Numbers 20:1–13; utilizing the spiritual sense, Kadesh is the church, having received faith and its characteristic "living waters." Although Lombard copied the *Glossa*'s claim that Jewish communities are ignorant of the true law and the Scriptures, he also demonstrates that he can interpret for himself, choosing anti-Jewish readings only when they suit him.

Hugh of St. Cher (d. 1263) continued the early Chrisitan tradition of linking God's voice to Jesus' preaching and echoed Bruno di Segni's claim that God's voice may also be heard through the preaching of the apostles and their successors. As a Dominican prelate, it is not surprising that he should have emphasized his own vocation here. Psalm 29:3 and 6 describe the good words of preachers that should return to their source (Gen 3:19) and call listeners to repentance (John 1:23) and good works (Mark 3:5; Prov 31:19). Psalm 29:4 refers to Jesus' preaching which brings about piety (Eccl 8:4; Matt 7:29), reverence for God, respect for parents, compassion for the less fortunate, and occassionally fear (1 Tim 4:7; Luke 11:39). Hugh interpreted Psalm 29:5 allegorically as a tale concerning humility and penance. Arrogant cedars, particularly the Jewish people, are subdued, although some will receive salvation (Isaiah 40:31). According to Hugh there are good cedars (Christ, virgins, angels, good clerics, philosophers, just individuals, the Israelites according to 2 Kgs 14:9, princes and the holy congregation) and bad cedars (the devil, arrogant and wicked individuals, and tyrants). It must be pointed out that Hugh's prooftexting often took place at the price of distorting the original meaning of his proofs. Therefore, one should not assume that the "presence" of scriptural "support" for his claims always equals sound exegesis.

Regarding God's voice in Psalm 29:6–9, Hugh shows off his ability to read first allegorically and then tropologically. Jesus although physically a Jew is not like the unicorns of verse 6, or the arrogant Jews who do not accept the New Testament. Those books, however, one day will destroy the horns of the stubborn unicorns. Continuing with the theme of destruction, God's voice in verse 7 either destroys the roots of sin before they turn into action or prevents the sinful act from becoming habitual. Sin itself can never be completely wiped out because that is not God's will. Hugh's proof here was Numbers 8:6. According to the verse, Levites must shave, not pluck, their body hair; this for Hugh was evidence that no thought may be eliminated completely. If the troublesome thought remains, however, it is not strong enough to turn into action. The first desert of Psalm 29:8 is the Gentiles who lack the Torah or the prophets but come to faith through God's spirit. The desert of Kadesh is the Jews, who lack the spirit. Now reading tropologically, God's voice refers to righteous indignation that motivates one to love God's word and avoid sin through listening to timely and effective preaching. Although God's voice will cut off the unfruitful (Matt 3:10) and cause fear (Hab 3:2; Acts 2:37), it also can facilitate repentance (Sir 12:12) and keep the sinful heart from remaining a barren, uncultivated desert (Prov 24:30–31; Isa 35:7). Bruno argues that the deer in Psalm 29:9 are preachers, but Hugh concludes that the deer are laity motivated by good preaching to serve God. Hugh's exegesis exemplifies the highs and lows of medieval Christian interpretation: Hermeneutical dexterity combined with anti-Judaism and a number of suspect prooftexts.

The last major exegete, Nicholas of Lyra (1270?–1340), cut through the layers of spiritual senses and emphasized the literal sense in his commentary. Although Nicholas argued that God's peace in Psalm 29:11 referred to the daily sacrifice of Jesus Christ as embodied in the sacrament of the Eucharist, God's voice refers to God's acts on Israel's behalf. These acts included the parting of the Red Sea and the subsequent destruction of the Egyptian horses and riders, as well as the giving of the Torah and Decalogue, which scared the Israelites so badly that they became too afraid to hear God's voice directly and insisted that Moses relay the messages to them instead. Nicholas observed that the Vulgate substitutes "unicorn" [*unicornium*] for "wild oxen" [*ben re'emim*] in verse 6, but concludes that the substitution does not change the verse's meaning. The Israelites remained terrified of God's voice, and only Moses was brave enough to listen to God. Verses 7 and 8 refer to Numbers 16 and the destruction of Korah, his friends, and their tabernacle through earthquake and fire. In the desert of Kadesh the Israelites wandered for forty years before entering the Promised Land.

Nicholas devoted most of his commentary space on Psalm 29 to verse 9. He noted that the Vulgate translation was a bit unusual, but decided to use it anyway. God's voice and virtue enable deer to have healthy pregnancies and deliveries now and in the future, against, in Nicholas's opinion, the Muslims [*tartaris et saracenis*] and any others who claimed that animals neither will need food nor be eaten themselves in the world to come. Nicholas concluded by mentioning Jerome's connection of Psalm 29:9 to Genesis 49's description of Naphtali, a deer that sings God's praises in a beautiful voice.

Like their Jewish counterparts, Christian interpreters generally used the psalm to preach, often about the benefits of sound Christian preaching, with proofs from other biblical texts added for good measure. Nicholas of Lyra is the exception, but he did continue the tradition of reading the psalm combatively. While his predecessors attacked Jews, Nicholas protested against Muslims and their unnamed theological allies. Even an emphasis upon the literal sense made room for polemic, raising the question of whether medieval Christian exegetes could interpret a Hebrew Bible text without including their own theological concerns.

The answer appears to be no, but the answer is the same if the question is directed to the rabbis at the beginning of this chapter. Medieval interpreters did not hesitate to bring their thoughts and ideas to the biblical text under examination. Although some modern exegetical methods encourage more objectivity, the rabbis and priests here are similar to rhetorical and ideological critics of the Bible who acknowledge that all language exists to make a point. Therefore, the primary question is whether the exegesis is persuasive, not whether it should be. In the case of the Christian scholars, the regularity with which interpretation comes at the expense of Judaism should be a warning against self-absorbed exegesis. Biblical stories are not inherently our stories and should not be read as if the reader and her biases are the center of the universe. All of the authors mentioned, however, agree that God's voice is a wonder to hear, suggesting that personal opinion aside, a psalm that praises God's voice is interpreted primarily as such. The garnish may vary, but the meal remains the same, regardless of who invites you to dine.

Bibliography

Bergeron, L. "Bruno de Segni." In *Dictionnaire de spiritualite* 1.2:1969.

Biblia Latina cum glossa Ordinaria: Facsimile Reprint of the Edition Princeps Adolph Rusch of Strassburg 1480/81. Edited by K. Froelich and M. I. Gibson. Brepols: Turnhout, 1992.

Biblia sacra iuxta Vulgatam versionem. 4th ed. Edited R. Gryson. Stuttgart: Deutsche Bibelgesellschaft, 1994.

Boyarin, Daniel. *Intertextuality and the Reading of Midrash*. Indiana Studies in Biblical Literature. Bloomington: Indiana University Press, 1990.
Bruno di Segni. *Opera Omnia: Tomus Primus: Expositio in Psalmos*. Patrologia Latina 164. Paris: Migne, 1884.
Evans, G. R. *The Language and Logic of the Bible*. Volume 1: *The Earlier Middle Ages*. Cambridge: Cambridge University Press, 1984.
———. *The Language and Logic of the Bible*. Volume 2: *The Road to Reformation*. Cambridge: Cambridge University Press, 1985.
Hugh of Saint-Cher. *Postillae super universum Vetus et Novum Testamentum*. Volume 1: *In libros Genesis–Job*. Germany: Coloniae Agrippinae, 1621.
Kimchi, David. *Ha-Perush ha-shalem 'al Tehilim*. Edited by A. Darom. Jerusalem: Mossad Harav Kook, 1967.
Lubac, Henri de. *Medieval Exegesis: The Four Senses of Scripture*. Volume 1. Translated by Mark Sebanc. Grand Rapids: Eerdmans, 1998.
———. *Medieval Exegesis: The Four Senese of Scripture*. Volume 2. Translated by E. M. Macierowski. Grand Rapids: Eerdmans, 2000.
Marcus, Jacob Rader. *The Jew in the Medieval World: A Source Book, 315–1791*. Rev. ed. Cincinnati: Hebrew Union College, 1999.
McKenzie, Steven L., and Stephen R. Haynes, eds. *To Each Its Own Meaning: An Introduction to Biblical Criticisms and Their Application*. Rev. ed. Louisville: Westminster John Knox, 1999.
Nicholas of Lyra. *Postilla Super Totam Bibliam III: Stasburg 1492*. Unveranderter Nachdruck. Frankfurt: Minerva, 1971.
Pearl, Chaim. *Rashi*. New York: Grove, 1988.
Peter Lombard. *Glossa in Psalterium*. Microfilm reproduction of British Library Ms. Additional 18299. 1478.
Rashi. *Parshandatha: ve-hu perush Rashi 'al nevi'im u ketuvim*, Vol. 3. Edited by I. Marsden. Jerusalem: Makor, 1936.
Rayez, Andre. "Hugues de Saint-Cher." In *Dictionnaire de spiritualite* 7.1:900.
Samuel ben Meir. *Sefer Tehillim: im Perush Rashbam*. Berlin: Holzinger, 1816.
Smalley, Beryl. *The Study of the Bible in the Middle Ages*. Notre Dame: University of Notre Dame Press, 1978.
Trebolle Barrera, Julio. *The Jewish Bible and the Christian Bible: An Introduction to the History of the Bible*. Translated by Wilfred G. E. Watson. Leiden: Brill, 1998.
Weiss Halivini, David. *Peshat and Derash: Plain and Applied Meaning in Rabbinic Exegesis*. New York: Oxford University Press, 1991.

7

Luther and Calvin Read Psalm 29

Lowell K. Handy

FOR THE THOUSAND YEARS PRIOR TO THE PROTESTANT REFORMATION Christian interpretation of the psalms had been founded in the Alexandrian School of Bible study. Any sacred text was understood to bear a variety of meanings. One of the aims of the protesting Christians was to put an end to this complicated manner of reading the church's sacred texts. For Protestants there was a firm belief that revelation from God ought to be clear to anyone who took time to read the text and put thought into its meaning. Therefore, it was a foundational belief of the movement that the literal meaning of the biblical text was authoritative and that the definitive text itself was the Hebrew, Aramaic, or Greek of the earliest manuscripts. The Latin translation used by the Catholic Church, the Vulgate, was conscientiously supplanted with translations into regional dialects. It was insisted that each (Protestant) Christian was capable of reading and understanding the word of God once a reliable translation into the vernacular language was made available. Some texts, however, could not be understood literally, but were clearly metaphors or allegories; this approach to the passages was assumed to be discernable from the Bible itself. Nonetheless, the meaning of even non-allegorical passages that had taken on Christian significance through the millennium and a half of the church was often retained. This was certainly true of the Psalms as read by both Calvin and Luther, each attempting to produce new Protestant readings of the psalms while simultaneously depending heavily on the earlier work of Jerome and Augustine.

Martin Luther

Martin Luther (1483–1546) was trained as a Bible scholar in the Augustinian order of monks to which he belonged. He first lectured on Psalms in the years 1513 through 1515. Having been trained in the manner of late medieval exegesis, Luther presented his lectures in the form of glosses and scholia. This meant that he selected the verses and words on which he wished to comment and then dealt with them often in isolation from the rest of the poem; for Luther these were mostly theologically important citations. From the variety of meanings current in the medieval interpretation of Scripture, Luther preferred to discourse on the "moral" meaning of Scripture (the *sensus tropologicus*). His early lectures for his commentary on the Psalms dealt heavily with their Christology; this approach continued an interpretation of Old Testament texts within Christianity popular since the early years of the church and was especially prevalent in the commentary on Psalms by Augustine himself. In this approach all anthropological references to God in the Old Testament were taken to be clear references to Jesus as the Second Person of the Trinity. Thus, in Psalm 29, "the voice of the Lord" was assumed, in agreement with almost all medieval Christian scholars, by Luther to be the voice of Jesus. That Luther's Psalms commentary was created early in his career means that it retained a close relationship to the medieval interpretation in which he had been trained. His later German translations of the psalms would more fully reflect a Protestant orientation.

Psalm 29 appears in Luther's first series of lectures on the Psalms, but not in the second (±1518), where he was more selective in his passages. The first lectures began with Psalm 1 and went straight through the psalms to Psalm 126, where the academic term ended for that year. It is clear that Luther began the series grounded in medieval Catholic Christology based on the Vulgate Bible; however, as he progressed through the psalms, his attention was increasingly attracted to the language of the Hebrew original. By the end of the lecture series Luther had abandoned both the Vulgate as his primary text and the Christocentric interpretation of the content; ancient Israel was by the end of the series the basis of meaning for the psalms. His shift in approach came after the lecture on Psalm 29, so the psalm provides a perfect example of how the psalm was read by Luther on the eve of his movement from "Catholic" to "Protestant" interpretation.

Luther loved the psalms. He cited them extensively in all his writings. But Psalm 29 was not one of his favorites and received few citations in his work. It even disappears as a citation in his Psalms commentary itself after a final reference to it on Psalm 32:2. However, it is interesting that the few references Luther made to the psalm once his break with Rome had become permanent show little change in his understanding of this particular poem. Other psalms, more often cited by Luther, clearly had changed in meaning for Luther as he matured.

Luther read Psalm 29 as an attack on heretics. He included among the groups being condemned Arians, Jews, those who are superstitious, and the *singularitas* (translated in Luther's Works as "individualists," meaning those who reject the church and create their own sense of right and wrong). All of these groups are defined as those who desired to live outside the church community, those with pride, those who live in the flesh (a transparent reference to Paul's epistles, to which Luther had a particular theological attachment), and those who simply prefer the devil to Christ. It should be noted that Luther was not always the most subtle or diplomatic of commentators. The psalm, then, for Luther, became a summons for all peoples to turn their praise to the true faith as found in the Christian God as embodied in the Second Person of the Trinity: the Son of God, Jesus as the risen Christ. The sole place to find this true God, Luther believed, was in the Christian church community, which, at the time of the first Psalms lecture series, he still believed was within the Roman Catholic Church properly understood. It is appropriate to accept that Luther read Psalm 29 primarily as a Christian supersessionist document; the Jews form its central concern with a Christian declaration that the church had superseded the synagogue as the community of God's salvation. In this Luther followed a long Christian tradition of interpreting Scripture extending back to the New Testament.

Luther's mentor in understanding the vocabulary of Psalm 29 was Augustine with additional material explicitly derived from Jerome. For this he was dependant primarily on the Latin of the Vulgate translation, still the authoritative text as he began his Psalms lecture series. Occasionally he would make comments about the Greek of the Septuagint or the Hebrew of the Jewish Bible. So, for example the "rams" of the Latin first verse do not appear in Hebrew versions of the psalm, but had appeared already in the Greek of the Septuagint prior to the

Latin translation. As these "rams" had become important for Christian theological readings of Psalm 29, Luther continued in that reading. As Augustine had defined these rams as being the faithful Christians, Luther accepted this metaphor. He then expanded the allusion by concentrating on the two horns on a ram's head, identifying them with the Old and New Testaments; these he perceived as the two weapons that all followers of Christ wield to fight the devil. When Luther turned from the Vulgate to the Hebrew, these rams disappeared and the Hebrew text became his basis for the 1524 translation of the phrase as *Kinder der Götter* (children of God), though clearly his understanding of this phrase to mean the Christian church had not changed.

Luther understood the second line of the psalm (still in verse one) to distinguish between glory and honor. Honor is that which is owed to one deserving reverence, while glory is that which is defused among the adoring throngs such that they will indeed honor one who is worthy of such honor. Glory, therefore, is an ever-expandable force that causes more and more people to honor the worthy person. Who is worthy to be honored by all humanity? It is the Son of God according to Luther. Since the "name" (and here Luther used a traditional Jewish theological understanding of the phrase *hashem*, "the name") could only refer to God and, in accordance with Augustine, it could only refer to the human God in the Second Person of the Trinity, one should honor Jesus. And here Luther turned to three Christian proof texts to support his interpretation of the "name." Exodus 23:21; Psalm 8:1; and Philippians 2:9 were used to demonstrate that God had bestowed the divine name on God the Son. The Philippians passage was also used to argue that this "name" designated the one who was above all others.

The "holy court" of verse two was understood to be the church founded by Jesus. Heretics, Jews, and others wish to remain outside the church, although Luther did credit them all with the desire to worship and honor God. However, it was Luther's contention that they cannot truly do so outside of God's own church community. Hence, the admonition was to those beyond the confines of the church to enter it and there properly worship.

The first of seven citations of "the voice of the Lord" appears in verse three. This phrase was used by Luther almost indistinguishably from the "word of the Lord," partly meaning Jesus (as in the prologue to the Gospel of John), but usually meaning the teachings of Jesus and/

or the Bible generally. This voice is "above the waters" and Luther again turned to Augustine to understand what this phrase meant. In this case Augustine had turned to 2 Samuel 14:14 and Revelation 17:15 to define the "waters" as signifying the people. Building on this, Luther chose three analogies between water and people: 1) we people have short lives, 2) we are not solid but swish around, and 3) we are buffeted by our inner desires. For Luther, then, the line meant that despite our less than sterling behavior, the "Voice of the Lord" stays with us over tumultuous lives, always waiting for us to pay attention.

The bulk of Luther's lecture on Psalm 29 concerned verse five. Here he took up the proper meaning of the terms "Lebanon" and "cedars." Basically, he understood "Lebanon" to refer to the Jews, or as he phrased it: "the people of the old law." In this he followed earlier Christian interpretations of Old Testament poetic passages where Lebanon had been assumed to be a clear reference to the Israelites as recipients of God's covenant. For Luther, then, that Lebanon meant the synagogue was a fixed Bible-based metaphor. "Cedars," on the other hand, he read in two different manners. As a purely negative reference, following Augustine, he accepted it as the standard metaphor representing pride; he admonishes his students to overcome their proclivity toward this sin with humility and patience. On the other hand, being possibly either a negative or positive attribute, "cedars" referred to the leaders of the people. These are those who stand over others as the elite and the exalted; for Luther it tended toward a negative connotation for rulers in general.

In verse six Luther explicitly followed Jerome, though it was earlier followed by Augustine as well, in reading "the calf of Lebanon" as a reference to Jesus' crucifixion. The parallel line, it might be noted, which came out in translation as the unicorn of Sirion, Luther identified with the rhinoceros and he retained this translation in his own German Psalter. For Luther, Jesus is the calf who is derived from the Jews that is to be slaughtered as a weakling offering in order to break the power and privilege of the proud and elite. He continued by remarking that the Jews are now (citing verse eight) untrue to their own savior and so known by the name of their heresy against God in Kadesh; in which he appears to have confused his Old Testament passages. The Jews, Luther insisted, lived by the flesh while Jesus showed the way to live by the spirit.

As for those fiery flames in verse seven, those, of course, were temptations! The "voice of the Lord" does not break forth in temptations, but breaks forth in order to suppress temptations. In verse nine the "hinds" were understood as yet another metaphor for the people of God while the forests were understood as the holy books of Christianity. Exactly how Luther leapt from the text, even in Latin, to an understanding of Christian study and meditation on the holy Scriptures in this passage Luther did not explain. His citations of biblical proof texts from the Song of Songs and 1 Corinthians do not really clarify the interpretation he made. Nonetheless, Luther explained verse nine as an admonition to bring up your "sons" by teaching and example.

When Luther concluded the lecture on Psalm 29, the calf, by way of extension from having been understood as referring to Jesus, was to be recognized as the people of the church who had developed from the synagogue. Those who are haughty, and Luther singled out the Jews here, have been broken to pieces so that only the humble remain. So, like those who had lived in the flesh now live in the spirit, so too only the humble before God remain.

The post-break-with-Rome Luther may well have switched to the Hebrew text of the psalm, as can be seen in his series of translations of Psalm 29, but still in the mid 1520s he read Psalm 29:9 as hinds calving (along with most other Christian translators, Catholic and Protestant), seeing it as a reference to the "voice of the Lord" (Jesus) confounding the "hinds" (people, or most explicitly the leaders of the people). This later interpretation came in a note concerning Hosea 8:10. More significant was Luther's reference to Psalm 29 in his 1538 treatise on the Sermon on the Mount where he cited the psalm to show how the "voice of the Lord" (God's word=Jesus Christ=Jesus' teachings) changes the entire world, humbling the kings and rulers, providing their only possible escape from hell and the devil, shattering their pride and disobedience. In fact, it reflects that, despite his shift in exegetical method, his understanding of Psalm 29 had not materially changed from that of fifteen years earlier.

John Calvin

Like innumerable others, John Calvin (1509–1564) early in the Protestant movement produced a collection of psalm translations. His appeared in 1539 as a joint work with Clement Marot. Marot was the poet in this pair and produced the final form of most of the psalms. Many Protestant congregations had restricted hymns in worship services to translations of the psalms and Protestants from all areas, whether their particular denomination was restricting itself to the singing of psalms or not, raced to produce vernacular psalm books and psalter hymnals. Even Protestant rulers were not immune from the psalm translating craze with King James the VI of Scotland and I of England producing a (really awful) Psalms translation, published posthumously by William Alexander in 1631, which mercifully the 1611 Psalms of the Authorized Version of the Bible (now usually known as The King James Version) kept from becoming the official psalter of the Church of England. Calvin, who had in fact been trained as a lawyer, held as his main concern the reordering of the church and the restoring of proper order and belief. He was determined that the psalms would be central in the worship service of his congregations. The various psalters that were produced for worship in the Reformed churches Calvin continued to monitor throughout his life, though he did not, after the first foray, attempt to produce another translation himself.

He did, however, have a great concern that the Protestants understand the psalms as God intended them to be read and for this he produced a commentary. Calvin's Psalms Commentary appeared first in 1557 in the *lingua franca* for scholars and clergy of the day, Latin. Since it was deemed necessary for all Christians to properly read Scripture, the French translation of the commentary appeared the following year, 1558. Unlike Luther's Lectures on the Psalms and, indeed, unlike other of Calvin's commentaries, this was a book written to be a commentary and was not transcriptions of lecture notes. His was a commentary in the modern sense of the word, dealing with each passage and each word in context and for its meaning within each psalm.

Calvin praised the work of some other Protestant commentators on the Psalms, but insisted that so far no one had attempted a commentary based solely on the text, not relying on Christian traditional interpretations and Christology. Calvin had learned Hebrew from Sebastian Münster in order to read the Old Testament in its original language and it was the Hebrew text that he took to be the sole authoritative basis for understanding the psalms. Calvin claimed a dual approach to recapturing the true meaning of Scripture: 1) noting the historical problem of errors introduced through the transmission of the text; and 2) taking into consideration the human imagination as having creatively corrupted the meaning of texts. His solution was to read the Hebrew text (with some corrections) relying on the Holy Spirit to guide the earnest Christian reader. While in theory Calvin vigorously denied allegorical meanings of texts, in practice he accepted typological understandings of some (and especially psalm) passages. For Calvin, if traditional Christian interpretations of the psalms were suspect, he made extensive use of classical poetry to comment on the psalms for the devotional thought of the ancient world from which the book of Psalms derived.

Like Luther, Calvin was thoroughly acquainted with the Vulgate (Latin) and Septuagint (Greek) versions of the psalms and could make use of them in his commentaries; however, for Psalm 29 he cited them only to show how far from the true Hebrew text they had strayed. He made clear in his introduction to the psalm that the psalm was written by King David in order to demonstrate God's omnipotence as manifested in nature. While he claims that the poem describes nature in a naturalistic fashion, he continued the church's traditional reading of the poem as a warning to proud and powerful humans. Unlike Luther, or the Christian traditional commentators, Calvin refused to read the psalm as Christology or to see in it a reference to the Christian rather than the Jewish community.

He began the commentary by observing that traditional Christian translations of Psalm 29:1 simply continue a misreading by Greek translators of the Hebrew text; there are no rams in the verse. He dismissed both Christian and Jewish commentators as having misunderstood the phrase and then translated the term in question quite literally (if as only one of several possible literal translations) as "sons of the mighty," which he took to refer to the "princes of this world," who were being summoned by David to humble themselves before God. The "strength" of the second line was taken to be the central point of the opening part of the psalm; princes of this world assume that they have their power by means of their own strength, but God alone is the source of all power. While Luther had taken the (still enigmatic) phrase *hadrath-qodesh* as a reference to the church, Calvin assumed an ancient Israelite allusion. Since David was writing the psalms before his son built the temple, Calvin deducted that the phrase denotes the Tabernacle. This was the one place of pure worship of God in David's time; it is not, Calvin went out of his way to explain, a reference to heaven.

Having taken care of what he deemed the preface to the poem, Calvin treated the body of the psalm as a description of the revelation of God in the wonders of nature. The "voice of God" was expansively explained to refer to thunder. Thunder is that aspect of the natural world that catches the attention of even the most powerful of rulers and the most lazy of intellectuals causing them, at least momentarily, to think of God. David, therefore, began the psalm with a bang, simultaneously terrifying and humbling the obstinate. David then repeated the voice in a powerful series of natural phenomena displaying the might of God in the face of the powerlessness of humanity.

The passages containing the "breaking of cedars" and "breaking the cedars of Lebanon" Calvin insisted refer to natural events, real trees and real mountains. The purpose of the violent images is to bring intellectuals and philosophers away from their "diabolical" reasonings and back to the proper awe for God. In the recitation of the storm imagery in Psalm 29 where Lebanon skips like a calf or Sirion like a unicorn, Calvin accepted that the poet made use of poetic license and hyperbole; and, yes, Calvin accepted the Hebrew text as referring to a unicorn (not Luther's rhinoceros), used, he assumed, because of the remarkable speed of the fabulous beasts. For the fiery flames, Calvin turned to Aristotle and explained the "science" of lightning bolts that accompany thunder ("voice of the Lord"). The admonition of the psalm was then understood to be that one should not fear thunderstorms, but the creator of thunderstorms.

He took time to explain why in Psalm 29:8–9 "to bring forth" is a bad translation of the Hebrew while "to tremble" was the correct one (an option still accepted). "Wilderness" he translated literally, but allowed that it may be by *synecdoche* (a literary metaphor using terms for large areas to refer to that which is therein contained) a reference to all the wild animals that lived in wilderness areas and thus a reference to all the animals mentioned in the psalm. The purpose of the body of the psalm for Calvin was to show that God is in control of nature and the entire world. The voice of the Lord is recognized by all of nature, but that humans do not notice the voice of God even though it is obvious and inescapable. That the voice penetrates even the forests illustrated for Calvin that God exists in even the most secret and hidden of places.

Calvin understood the "temple" of verse 9 to be the church or the Jewish temple. It is there that the word of God is properly proclaimed; Calvin, like Luther, took the voice of the Lord here to refer to Scriptures rightly taught and properly revered. When all say "Glory!" the congregants consecrate themselves to the service of God. It is noteworthy that Calvin called Christians to the service of God rather than to the worship of God in that Calvin asked a great deal of his Protestants in a social setting. For Calvin central to the word of God was the doctrine of salvation and central to accepting salvation is to recognize that the revelation of God's truth was to Judea, alone of all the peoples on earth.

The conclusion of Psalm 29 finds God enthroned above the flood. Calvin insisted that this was not intended as a threat of another Noatic Flood, but a reminder that God is ruler above the very strongest force in nature. God is the eternal power, superior to anything in nature or among humans. Calvin went on to argue that God is powerful enough to curb any violent divine urge to punish humanity again in the manner of the flood here represented. In the end, Calvin insisted, God supports the elect people not in fear but in peace. All that is necessary for the needs of a godly population comes from God. All who live in accordance with the humility proper before the omnipotent deity displayed in the power of nature will live happy and prosperous lives. In the end the people of God are defended by the infinite power of God, creator and controller of the entire world.

Calvin did not make a great use of Psalm 29 in his numerous writings. In his Sermons on Job the psalm is cited both as referring to the word of God as the object of devotion and to the God who brings peace and prosperity to the elect people. The latter notion from the psalm also is mentioned in the Sermons on Samuel along with the psalm's presentation of tempests as a sign of God's power. In a study of Exodus Calvin also notes Psalm 29:2 regarding God's presence in the tabernacle.

In the end it might be pointed out that while Luther retained throughout his life a supersessionalist reading of Psalm 29, Calvin was accused throughout his career and well after his death of leaving the door open for the salvation of Jews on their own merit. This certainly may be seriously claimed of his commentary on Psalm 29 where he explicitly declares Judea unique in the world as the recipient of God's saving message while totally discarding the supersessionalist rhetoric of his tradition and his peers. In this Calvin appears much more the modern exegete of Psalm 29 than does Luther.

Bibliography

Armstrong, Brian G. "Report on the Seminar: An Investigation of Calvin's Principles of Biblical Interpretation." *HvTSt* 54 (1998) 133–42.

Aurelius, Carl Axel. "Luther on the Psalter." *LQ* 14 (2000) 193–205.

Bainton, Roland. *Here I Stand: A Life of Martin Luther.* Nashville: Abingdon, 1950.

Black, C. Cliffton, III. "Unity and Diversity in Luther's Biblical Exegesis: Psalm 51 as a Test-Case." *SJT* 38 (1985) 325–45.

Calvin, John. *Commentary upon the Book of Psalms.* Edited and translated by James Anderson. Grand Rapids: Eerdmans, 1949.

Greef, Wulfert de. "Calvin as Commentator on the Psalms." In *Calvin and the Bible*, edited by Donald K. McKim, 85–106. Cambridge: Cambridge University, 2006.

Hall, Basil. "Biblical Scholarship: Editions and Commentaries." In *The Cambridge History of the Bible: The West from the Reformation to the Present Day*, edited by S. L. Greenslade, 39–140. Cambridge: Cambridge University Press, 1963.

Holladay, William L. *The Psalms through Three Thousand Years: Prayerbook of a Cloud of Witnesses.* Minneapolis: Fortress, 1993.

Parker, T. H. L. *John Calvin: A Biography.* London: Dent, 1975.

Preus, James S. "Old Testament *Promissio* and Luther's New Hermeneutic." *HTR* 60 (1967) 145–61.

Lestringant, Frank. "Calvin et Marot, ou de l'universalité des psaumes." In *Calvin et ses contemporains: Actes du colloque de Paris 1995*, edited by O. Millet, 247–60. Geneva: Droz, 1998.

Luther, Martin. *First Lectures on the Psalms. Volume I: Psalms 1–75.* Edited by Hilton C. Oswald. Luther's Works 10. St. Louis: Concordia, 1974.

Roussel, Bernard. "Des auteurs." In *Les temps des Réformes et la Bible*, edited by Guy Bedouelle and Bernard Roussel, 199–282. BTT 5. Paris: Beauchesne, 1989.

———. "Des protestants." In *Les temps des Réformes et la Bible*, edited by Guy Bedouelle and Bernard Roussel, 309–25. BTT 5. Paris: Beauchesne, 1989.

———. "Les deux derniers tiers du siècle." In *Les temps des Réformes et la Bible*, edited by Guy Bedouelle and Bernard Roussel, 125–56. BTT 5. Paris: Beauchesne, 1989.

Stewart, Alan. *The Cradle King: The Life of James VI & I, the First Monarch of a United Great Britain.* New York: St. Martin's, 2003.

Zachman, Randall C. "Gathering Meaning from the Text: Calvin's Exegetical Method." *JR* 82 (2002) 1–26.

8

The Liturgical Use of Psalm 29

Bert Polman

AS THIS VOLUME DEMONSTRATES, THE SCHOLARLY LITERATURE ON Psalm 29 is extensive and based on a large body of psalm studies from the previous half-century. Scholars such as Mitchell Dahood, Peter Craigie and Carola Kloos have focused on the relationship between the biblical text of Psalm 29 and other ancient Near Eastern texts, especially those from the Canaanite region into which the Hebrews settled after their exodus from Egypt. The highly symmetrical use of the terms "Lord" and the "voice of the Lord" in this psalm has fascinated scholars for years. David Noel Freedman and C. Franke-Hyland are representatives of those who have put this psalm text through a rigorous structural poetic analysis, while Pieter M. Venter, more recently, updates such an analysis with special attention to the physical and symbolic places mentioned in the body of the psalm. Less attention has been paid to the liturgical functions of Psalm 29 in the Judeo-Christian tradition and it is this latter topic that is the focus of this specific chapter. How was and is Psalm 29 used in Jewish worship past and present? And how do the various Christian traditions (Eastern Orthodox, Roman Catholic and Protestant) make use of this psalm text in traditional and contemporary worship?

Psalm 29 in Jewish Worship

Numerous scholars have categorized Psalm 29 as a victory hymn, analogous to the Song of the Sea (Exod 15:1–18; also called the Song of Moses), the Song of Deborah (Judg 5) and the Song of Hannah (1 Sam 2:1–10). Are these early song examples from the *Book of the Wars of the Lord* mentioned in Numbers 21:14? And was Psalm 29 actually initially a part of that otherwise virtually unknown collection? Why was the Exodus 15 hymn not incorporated into the Book of Psalms? Were such songs used in the Tabernacle during the Hebrew desert travels, or at least prior to the installation of temple worship in Jerusalem? These are fascinating questions, but they remain unanswered and unanswerable given the absence of sufficient details.

Equally evocative, but also inconclusive for the question of how Psalm 29 was used in early Jewish worship, is the relationship between the Hebrew text of this psalm and that of other ancient Near Eastern texts. Carola Kloos argued that the Hebrew God YHWH was assigned the traits of the Canaanite god Baal from earliest times, as in well before the prophets' denouncements of the Baal religion (Kloos, 124). This could presume an early dating for Psalm 29. However, Craigie claims that this psalm is strongly polemical, presumably contemporary with the later Hebrew prophets' attack against Baal. He suggests that Psalm 29 not only affirms YHWH as the Lord of nature and of the natural forces otherwise attributed to Baal, but that the text actually mocks those Baal powers (Craigie, 249). As the geographic origin of this psalm text is thought to be northern Canaan (given its references to Lebanon and Sirion [Mount Hermon]), there are speculations that the psalm may have its antecedents or analogues in Baal worship at Dan which was located just south of Mount Hermon in northern Canaan, but that this text was written or adapted for use in the orthodox worship of YHWH in Jerusalem's temple, possibly under the prodding of a "righteous" king such as Hezekiah or Josiah.

Equally elusive is the conjecture that Psalm 29 was used in a specific festival in the practices of Judean pre-Jewish worship related in the Hebrew Bible. The great form-critical scholars of the psalms, Hermann Gunkel and Sigmund Mowinckel had proposed an Autumn Festival or an Enthronement Festival in which they located the *Sitz im Leben* ("situation in life") of many psalms in the cultic rituals and festivals of Judean worship. In their view Psalm 29 becomes a royal psalm in which YHWH is the king. Similarly, Arthur Weiser proposed an annual Covenant Festival in which he claims many of the psalms find their function; he suggests Psalm 29 is a "theophany" psalm that signaled the appearance of God at such a festival. While most modern scholars of the psalms readily admit their profound debt to these form-critical scholars, there is a growing consensus that the evidence for such specific festivals is either exaggerated or certainly elusive and thus that any role that Psalm 29 may have had in such presupposed Enthronement or Covenant festivals is highly conjectural.

The Greek translation of the Hebrew Bible by the "Seventy" (thus LXX, or "Septuagint") adds a phrase to Psalm 29's customary superscription, "a psalm of David," concerning "the conclusion of Tabernacles." Various early Talmudic commentaries show that Psalm 29 was allied to the Feast of Tabernacles, *Sukkot*, either as one of the psalm readings for the opening of this autumn harvest festival or for use on the last day of this festival, typically sung at the dramatic moment in the service when the Torah scroll is returned to the Ark after the congregation has read from it. *Sukkot* celebrations focus on thanksgiving for the harvest (and by extension, how God took care of his people during their desert journey), and include prayers for rain (for which the thunderstorm in Psalm 29 fits well). The seven occurrences of the "voice of the Lord" in the body of the psalm are thought to correspond to the pouring of water on the seventh day of this feast, to the seven-day length of this event, and to the seven processions around the altar that occur during this time. The Septuagint's addition of "the Tabernacles" phrase presumably reflects contemporary Jewish practices of the Second Temple up to the time of its destruction in 70 CE. One may conjecture that Jesus would have been familiar with the use of Psalm 29 during his participation in the Feast of Tabernacles as recorded in John 7. While various Jewish sources attest to the use of Psalm 29 during the autumn Feast of Tabernacles, the important *Soferim* treatise (±600 CE) assigns Psalm 29 to the late spring Festival of Weeks, *Shavuot* or Pentecost (Elbogen, 115), which is the earlier of the two big harvest festivals. It is this *Shavuot* tradition which the great eleventh-century Rabbi Solomon ben Isaac (known as Rashi) follows when he interprets psalm 29 with reference to the giving of the law by God to Moses, which is a central theme of *Shavuot*; however, he makes no reference to the Feast of Tabernacles (Solomon ben Isaac, 150–52).

Modern Jewish use of Psalm 29 continues in the annual Feast of Tabernacles and in the weekly *Kabbalat Shabbat* ("Welcome to the Sabbath") which occurs each Friday in the late afternoon or around sundown as a precursor to the regular Friday evening service. The *Kabbalat Shabbat* service originated among Jewish mystics or kabbalists in the sixteenth-century. The contents of this service varies from one region and/or style of Judaism to another (Sephardic, Ashkenazic, Orthodox, Reform), but it is common for this part of the normal synagogue service to involve the readings of Psalms 95–99 and Psalm 29. These royal psalms emphasize the reign of the Lord and the six psalms together are thought to correspond to the six days of creation or to the six weekdays.

Among the usual components of the evening [*maariv*] or morning [*shacharit*] services are the *Shema* (Deut 6:4), with its blessings of creation, revelation and redemption; the series of *Amidah* prayers (which can be as many as eighteen "Benedictions," the first three of which are related to phrases in Psalm 29; the mourner's *Kaddish*; and several songs, including the famous kabbalists' hymn, *Lekhah Dodi* ("Come, My Friend") which welcomes the Sabbath as a bride. In addition, all of Psalm 29, or the "voice of the Lord" segments thereof, are often featured during the processing of the Torah in conjunction with the reading of the Jewish Scriptures.

Psalm 29 [28] in Eastern Orthodox Worship

The many translations into vernacular languages of the book of Psalms used in Eastern Orthodox Christian services derive from the Septuagint Greek translation. Since the Septuagint used a slightly different numbering system than the Hebrew Bible, Psalm 29 in the Hebrew text is Psalm 28 in most Bible versions used in the Eastern Orthodox churches. In the following section on Orthodox liturgy "Psalm 29" will be used in conformity with the Hebrew and Protestant Bibles numbering system; however, in the Orthodox traditions themselves this psalm is numbered "28."

As in Jewish tradition it is customary that portions of Psalm 29 are used as psalm versicles [*prokeimena*] in the Divine Liturgy and in the Matins of the Orthodox Church. Most common are verse 1: "Ascribe to the Lord..."; verse 3: "The voice of the Lord is over the waters..."; and verse 11: "The Lord will give strength to his people..." Such versicles usually precede the reading of a portion of Scripture and function much in the same way as the gradual does in the Roman Catholic mass.

But the most notable place for Psalm 29 in Orthodoxy occurs during the "Great Blessing of Water" (*megas agiasmos*), which is part of the Feast of Theophany or Epiphany. Since the early period of the church, Eastern Orthodoxy celebrated the baptism of Jesus on the day of Epiphany, January 6. That festival commemorates the manifestation of the Holy Trinity in that baptismal event: God the Father spoke "this is my Son" as Christ was baptized by John in the Jordan River during which time the Holy Spirit was symbolized by a dove descending on Jesus. Orthodox liturgy does not only emphasize the Trinity in the feast, however, but also focuses on the sanctification of water by the Spirit of God as explained by such church fathers as Saints Basil and Ambrose. According to Orthodox theology all creation is sanctified in Christ's baptism and thus it is fitting that a creation psalm such as Psalm 29, with its imagery of a storm, is an important part of the liturgy of Epiphany.

The "Great Blessing of Water" is held on the eve of the Feast of the Epiphany, during the "third royal hour" and has roots that date back to the compilation work of Saint Sophronius (560–638), who was the Patriarch of Jerusalem in his final years. The liturgy consists of Isaiah 35 and 55; 1 Corinthians 10:1–4; Mark 1:9–11; Psalms 29, 42 [=41], and 51 [=50]; and a number of prayers, including a special prayer for the sanctification of water by the Spirit of God. Because many more people are present for worship on the day of Epiphany, this service of the "Great Blessing of Water" is often repeated following the Divine Liturgy for Epiphany. After the solemn blessing the holy water is distributed to the church members for them to drink as a memorial of their own baptism and to be taken with them as blessing for their homes. With the words of Psalm 29 ringing fresh in their ears, Orthodox Christians practice what Saint John Chrysostom (347–407) taught in a sermon on the Epiphany: "For this is the day on which he was baptized and sanctified the nature of the waters. Hence for this reason during this feast at midnight we all, having drawn the water, deposit the streams at home and we keep it there for a whole year, in as much as it was on this day that the waters were sanctified." [*In homiliam de baptismo Christi et de epiphania* 2 [Migne PG 49.365–66], translated by Margaret M. Mitchell).

Psalm 29 in Western Christianity

As noted, the Eastern Church celebrates the baptism of Jesus on the Feast of the Epiphany. By contrast, the Western Church observes the coming of the Magi on Epiphany and celebrates the Baptism of the Lord on the Sunday after Epiphany. Also, note that the Vulgate Bible was based on the Septuagint and until modern times the Catholic Church has, like Orthodoxy, numbered Psalm 29 as Psalm 28; the most modern English Catholic Bibles have, however, adopted the Hebrew Bible numbering system.

While the medieval church in the west also assigned Psalm 29 to the service that focused on the baptism of Christ during the Epiphany season, it is the weekly chanting of this psalm that stands out in the medieval Roman Catholic tradition. In the monastic breviary (that is: the liturgy book of the daily Offices) of the later medieval times, Psalm 29 is one of a dozen psalms appointed to Matins for each Sunday morning in the ferial psalter, that is for ordinary week-days, not during the festive seasons (Harper, 259). In the ferial psalter for use outside of monastic institutions (for secular use), Psalm 29 appears among the psalms appointed for Matins of each Monday morning (Harper, 258). Reforms of the breviary in the sixteenth-century, in 1911 under Pope Pius X, and following the Second Vatican Council of the 1960s have produced changes in which psalms are assigned to which of the daily Offices, but the practice of reading or chanting the entire psalter in a week has continued largely unabated. Imagine singing Psalm 29 once a week throughout a person's entire adult lifetime!

Judiciously adopting and adapting various Roman Catholic and some Lutheran sources, Thomas Cranmer prepared the *Book of Common Prayer* for the young Anglican Church in 1549. Abandoning the weekly singing of the psalms during the eight daily Offices, he assigned the entire psalter to a monthly cycle, divided between Matins and Evensong. Psalm 29 was the third psalm appointed to Evensong on the fifth day of each month, following Psalms 27 and 28 (Harper, 265). The order of singing the psalms in the 1549 *Book of Common Prayer* was retained in the tables in the 1552, 1559, and 1662 editions, and survives largely unchanged in modern versions of the *Book of Common Prayer*. The various prayer-books that are used in Anglican churches world-wide today contain similar charts that promote this practice of singing all the psalms every month, including Psalm 29 in its appointed sequence.

John Calvin's emphasis on congregational singing of psalms produced the "Genevan" Psalter in 1562: *Les Psalmes mis en rime françoise par Clement Marot et Theodore de Beze*. Various charts are available from Calvin's church in Geneva which show the psalms, paraphrased in French, assigned to be sung on Sunday mornings and evenings and at Wednesday prayer meetings. The 1549 chart, when the "Genevan"

Psalter was still incomplete, covers some 50 psalms on a 17-week cycle and does not contain Psalm 29. Psalm 29 does appear on the 1553 chart that covers 83 psalms on a 28-week rotation; it is assigned there for Sunday evenings in the sixth week. Upon completion of the "Genevan" Psalter, the 1562 chart covers all 150 psalms on a 25-week cycle. In it Psalm 29 is now appointed to be sung early Sunday mornings ("at the ringing of the second bell") in each third week of this semi-annual rotation (Pidoux, 2.135).

The various *Kirchenordnung* (church order) documents of early Lutheranism appointed psalms to be sung in Latin or German for Matins and Vespers. Early Methodists tended to use the order of psalms assigned in the *Book of Common Prayer*. Without monastic institutions, however, only the Offices of Matins and Vespers, with their respective repertory of psalms, have prevailed among Protestant Christians and certainly not uniformly among them. While some local churches faithfully continue the practice of morning and evening Offices for the handful of people who come for such corporate daily worship, for many Christians the daily Offices have become simplified to their personal or family devotions. To that end various modern prayer-books and hymnals include charts and assign the psalms to be read daily at home, in various sequences, as a domestic or personal imitation of the traditional ordering of singing the psalms in corporate daily worship at church or monastery/convent. Any Christian who accepts that discipline of daily devotion will be confronted regularly with "the voice of the Lord" as Psalm 29 purports.

Psalm 29 in the Modern Ecumenical Lectionary of the West

Following the Second Vatican Council, the Roman Catholic Church produced a new lectionary in 1969. It was soon adopted and altered by Presbyterians, Anglicans, and Lutherans, as well as adopted for trial use in several other denominations in North America and, to a lesser extent, in other English-speaking countries. A process towards lectionary consensus was begun in 1978 by the Consultation on Common Texts. This resulted in the three-year *Common Lectionary*, published in 1983. After two cycles of use and many suggestions and criticisms, *The Revised Common Lectionary* was issued in 1992. Though *The Revised*

Common Lectionary is a widely accepted ecumenical text, there are still minor differences between *The Revised Common Lectionary* and the actual lectionary systems that prevail among Roman Catholics, Anglicans, Lutherans, Presbyterians, and Methodists.

The Revised Common Lectionary includes 105 psalms and 10 canticles as the responses to the first reading for each Sunday and feast-day, which is typically an Old Testament reading. As was noted in the descriptions above for the association of Psalm 29 with the baptism of Jesus, *The Revised Common Lectionary* appoints Psalm 29 among the following readings for the Epiphany Sunday devoted to the Baptism of the Lord:

Year A: Isaiah 42:1–9; Psalm 29; Acts 10:34–43; Matthew 3:13–17

Year B: Genesis 1:1–5; Psalm 29; Acts 19:1–7; Mark 1:4–11

Year C: Isaiah 43:1–17; Psalm 29; Acts 8:14–17; Luke 3:15–17, 21–22

In addition, Psalm 29 is assigned to Trinity Sunday in Year B in *The Revised Common Lectionary*; the usage of this psalm for the Trinity Festival was inherited from earlier Anglican traditions, though the relationship of Psalm 29 to the Feast of Trinity is clearly rooted in Eastern Orthodoxy's ancient emphasis on the Trinity at the baptism of Jesus.

Conclusion

Psalm 29 continues to hold an important place in both Jewish and Christian liturgies. Select portions of this psalm have found their appointed places in a variety of worship orders. The entire psalm has an honored place in the Jewish Feast of Tabernacles (*Sukkot*) and in the various Christian celebrations of the baptism of Jesus. And thus, "the voice of the Lord" continues to sound "upon the waters."

Bibliography

Craigie, Peter C. *Psalms 1–50*. WBC 19. Waco, TX: Word, 1983.
Dahood, Mitchell. *Psalms I: 1–50*. AB 16. Garden City, NY: Doubleday, 1966.
Elbogen, Ismar. *Jewish Liturgy: A Comprehensive History*. Translated by Raymond P. Scheindlin. Philadelphia: Jewish Publication Society, 1993.
Farrow, Michael G. *Psalms Verses of the Orthodox Liturgy: According to the Greek and Slav Usages*. Torrance, CA: Oakwood, 1997.
Ferguson, Everett. "Preaching at Epiphany: Gregory of Nyssa and John Chrysostom on Baptism and the Church." *CH* 66 (1997) 1–17.
Freedman, David Noel, and C. Franke Hyland. "Psalm 29: A Structural Analysis." *HTR* 66 (1973) 237–56.
Harper, John. *The Forms and Orders of Western Liturgy*. Oxford: Clarendon, 1991.
Kloos, Carola. *YHWH's Combat with the Sea: A Canaanite Tradition in the Religion of Ancient Israel*. Leiden: Brill, 1986.
Kraus, Hans-Joachim. *Psalms 1–59: A Commentary*. Translated by Hilton C. Oswald. Continental Commentaries. Minneapolis: Augsburg, 1988.
Pidoux, Pierre. *Le Psautier Huguenot de XVIe Siecle*. Vol. 2. Basel: Baerenreiter, 1962.
The Revised Common Lectionary. Winfield, BC: Wood Lake, 1992.
Solomon ben Isaac. *Rashi's Commentary on Psalms 1–89 (Books I–III)*. Translated and annotated by Mayer I. Gruber. SFSHJ 161. Atlanta: Scholars, 1998.
Venter, Pieter M. "Spaciality in Psalm 29." In *Psalms and Liturgy*, edited by Dirk J. Human and Cas J. A. Vos, 235–50. JSOTSup 410. London: T. & T. Clark, 2004.

9

Singing Psalm 29 Faithfully

Emily R. Brink

THE PSALMS CAN BE STUDIED, OR PROCLAIMED, OR PRAYED—OR SUNG. It is possible to study, preach, or pray the psalms without singing them. It is also possible to sing the psalms without studying or intentionally praying them. But the very act of singing the psalms is an act of proclamation, and it is in singing that the psalms have most deeply penetrated the hearts of God's people in every time and place. Singing the psalms provides the opportunity to both pray and proclaim God's word communally.

Singing the psalms has been characteristic of both Jewish and Christian worship. In the Jerusalem temple psalmody was part of an elaborate liturgy, connected to sacrifice, performed by highly trained Levite musicians, and accompanied by the softer stringed instruments that would not cover, but support the text (Stapert, 153). Not much is known about singing the psalms in early synagogues and churches, but psalmody became a regular part of the Latin Mass and a very important part of the monastic tradition, with all 150 psalms chanted weekly or monthy in the eight daily Offices, which are liturgies at set times throughout each day, beginning with matins and lauds and ending with compline. The practice of singing the psalms became largely a monastic and clerical practice, not one involving the laity.

The practice of singing the psalms changed dramatically in the sixteenth century Protestant Reformation with the introduction of metrical psalmody for the whole congregation to sing in the daily language of the people rather than in Latin. However, practices varied widely and even among those who for a couple of centuries sang *only* psalms in public worship, the rise of the English hymn tradition in the eighteenth century resulted in a gradual decline of psalmody. In the nineteenth and twentieth centuries singing the psalms virtually disappeared in many Protestant churches.

Practice changed dramatically again with the reforms of the Second Vatican Council (1962–1966) that stressed the role of the entire assembly in singing the psalms. Since then psalmody has received a great deal of attention among Roman Catholics and Protestants alike. The interest has been both ecumenical and world-wide, centered in singing the psalms communally in the common language of the people. As Roman Catholics worked at new ways of providing vernacular settings of the psalms, many Protestants restored or for the first time introduced psalmody to their regular order of worship, and many poets and composers were stimulated to provide fresh new settings. This renewal of interest in psalmody became part of a "hymn explosion" in the Western world, followed by a "hymnal explosion," and more recently in what could even be called a kind of "psalter explosion." Many psalm collections have been published in the last generation and recent hymnals in North America have greatly increased their inclusion of psalms, often in large psalm sections and in a variety of styles. The accessibility of all these new psalm settings does not necessarily mean that the practice of singing the psalms has increased, but in many traditions the practice has indeed been introduced or revived and renewed.

There are many ways to sing the psalms, and the structures of the psalms themselves suggest varied approaches. Given the need for repetition in order for people to sing a text of any length, what kind of structure can best help the singer live into the psalms? This chapter explores three basic ways that the psalms have been sung in public worship: in chant, in meter, and responsorially. Each way will be examined for its potential to pray and proclaim Psalm 29. In brief, the main distinctions among chanted, metrical, and responsorial psalmody are these:

- In chanted psalmody the music accommodates the text; that is, the psalm text is preserved and is sung to repeated adaptable melodic formulas.

- In metrical psalmody the text accommodates the music; that is, the poetic meter and melody are preserved, and the psalm text is adapted to fit that meter and repeated melody.

- In responsoral psalmody the psalm text is preserved, sung or read in sections by one person or an ensemble; surrounding those sections the entire congregation sings a short antiphon (or refrain) that highlights a key idea of the psalm.

How then should Psalm 29 be sung? It has been and continues to be sung in all three ways as outlined above. The question is also liturgical, cultural and ecumenical. Different types of psalmody stand in different liturgical traditions that have been shaped culturally and, especially in the last half century, ecumenically as well. Although there are beautiful settings of the psalms for solo and choral performance, the premise of this chapter is that congregational singing of the psalms should be primary, the root from which all other practices grow.

Chanting Psalm 29

The chant tradition is the oldest. One might ask: if the psalms are part of Scripture, would not the exact text take priority? Would not chant be the obvious choice? For those who honor Scripture as the inspired Word of God, especially those who speak of *sola scriptura*, why not keep the texts exactly as found in Scripture? This was the only way the psalms were sung communally for 1500 years in the western Christian tradition until the Reformation. The psalms still are chanted in Orthodox churches with chant melodies as aural icons that serve to transmit the psalm texts. Continuing the ancient traditions of the church, Orthodox pratice includes singing the entire psalter each week in daily services, though most people participate in services only on Sundays.

Three questions need to be asked when considering chant. First, what language should be used? Chant is so closely related to speech that it is very difficult to simply translate a language and expect it to fit the simple chant melodies that grew out of another language. Latin remained the unifying language of the Roman Catholic Church until the last third of the twentieth century, and Gregorian chant was preserved as long as Latin was retained. There is great power in unity of language across time and culture, as witness the use of Arabic for Islam, but Christianity has always become incarnate in particular times and places, and the gospel was translated from the earliest times into local languages. The second question is closely related to the first: what translation is best for singing? That is a different question than what is a good translation for reading or studying. The Latin translation of the psalms was born in chant more than in reading. The proliferation of new Scripture translations today aspire to understandability, faithfulness to the original Hebrew meanings, accessible vocabulary, and to being read aloud, not to being chanted. The third question is this: who does the singing? Speaking now only of the Roman Catholic tradition, chanting of the psalms in Latin was preserved by monks and clegy; the people did not sing or understand what was being sung.

Martin Luther and John Calvin both addressed these questions as they sought to reform worship practices and encourage congregational singing in the vernacular. The old struggles between tradition and reformation played out differently in the Lutheran and Calvinist traditions. Luther's tradition was one of chant; as a Benedictine monk he sang through the whole book of psalms in Latin weekly or monthly so he knew them by heart. He loved and wanted to preserve this heritage, even attempting to retain the Gregorian chant melodies, but he lamented that the German language just did not fit those tones. Luther's great contribution was to metrical hymnody: the great chorales that are still sung today, some based on the psalms. "A Mighty Fortress Is Our God" (to the tune EIN' FESTE BURG) is based on Psalm 46. Some have criticized this metrical setting as not being faithful to the psalm text, but Luther had no intention of considering this a psalm. Rather, he did what became a hallmark of Lutheran hymnody: he preached a sermon on Psalm 46 in "Ein feste Burg." To this day sermons are often followed with a hymn related to the preached text.

The power of the Lutheran chorale ended up eclipsing the tradition of chanted psalmody. Only in the past fifty years has psalmody once more received serious attention among Lutherans. To make a distinction between the psalms and their rich heritage of chorales, they turned again to chant, and this time it appears to be catching on as a practice for the entire congregation, though in a manner that has remained distinctly Lutheran and has not been adopted by other traditions. Even among Lutherans in North America there is no consensus on Scripture versions or psalm tones (chant meoldies). In every Lutheran hymnal since the groundbreaking *Book of Lutheran Worship* in 1978, psalm texts have been included, marked for singing in unison according to various given psalm tones. In Lutheran psalmody everyone sings everything in what would be called "direct psalmody."

In sixteenth century England another tradition of chanted psalmody began when Anglicans began choral singing of the psalms in English. Psalm tones expanded from unison singing to four-part harmony, often sung antiphonally, with choirs on both sides of a divided chancel singing responsively. This tradition has been preserved in Anglican and Episcopal cathedrals where choirs of men and boys still sing the psalms; many tourists have enjoyed attending evensong (vespers) to hear the psalms sung. Several cathedral choirs have recorded the psalms sung to chants from a host of composers dating from the sixteenth to the twenty-first centuries. This tradition has most often been reserved for choirs, not for congregational singing, though some Anglican congregations regularly chant the psalms in harmony. The practice of responsive *reading* of the psalms has become common for congregational use.

The great advantage of chanting the psalms is that they preserve the exact words of Scripture and honor the distinctive structure of Hebrew poetry with its vivid and concrete images, similes and metaphors. Though translations cannot preserve the assonance, alliteration, and wordplays of Hebrew, they do preserve the parallelism characteristic of Hebrew poetry. Most verses consist of pairs, and chants similarly are paired in two balanced sections, often separated with a semicolon. Most of the syllables are sung to one tone, perhaps with an initial "uptake" pitch to that held tone, and then with a marking indicating to move for the last couple of syllables to a closing cadence of two or three notes. Each verse repeats that pattern. Psalm 29 starts out this way in *Evangelical Lutheran Worship*, the 2006 successor to the 1978 *Lutheran Book of Worship*:

> Ascribe to the / LORD, you gods; ascribe to the LORD glo- / ry and strength.
>
> Ascribe to the LORD the glory / due his name; worship the LORD in the beau- / ty of holiness.

Each half starts out on a pitch that is held until the mark indicates a move toward the close of that phrase, the first half ends with a semicolon, the second half with a period. Rather than following a particular translation the psalms are punctuated in this format, prepared with singing in mind. Sometimes a "double chant" will involve four musical phrases which in effect forms a more hymn-like musical structure.

Several psalm tones are provided in Lutheran hymnals, and Anglican chants by various composers abound. The choice is up to the individual congregation with the understanding that not all tones match the mood of a given psalm. In theory, congregations have a variety of tones to choose from; in practice, many congregations have learned only one or two psalm tones and end up singing all the psalms to the same one or two formulas.

The great advantage of chanted psalmody is that it preserves the exact biblical text; the melodies are in service to the text. Specific words can be emphasized or lingered over slightly; dynamics can increase or decrease for emphasis. Just as a good reader declaims the text with attention to meaning, so good chanting brings out the meaning. Chant well done has an austere beauty. Chanting is also intriguingly counter-cultural, requiring only voices, preferably in resonant spaces that are kind to the voice, with only unobtrusive accompaniment that offers discreet support without drawing attention to itself.

There are also disadvantages to chant. In addition to the need for good acoustics and the time required to develop familiarity with this counter-cultural practice, there are limits to the abilities of most congregations to learn more than a few chant formulas. In practice, a few chants serve for the entire book of psalms. Psalms of praise, like Psalm 29, should sound different from psalms of lament or any other type of psalm; singing every psalm the same way robs the different psalm types of their distinct character and the individual psalms of their varied structures. Another disadvantage is the infrequency of chanting the psalms communally. The monastic pattern of singing many psalms every day helped greatly to preserve the tradition. Covering all the psalms in a month would mean singing about five psalms a day. Most people today sing perhaps one psalm a week in public worship, so it would take about three years to cover the psalms, if indeed they would all be sung. The *Revised Common Lectionary*, following a three-year pattern of Scripture readings, does not even include all the psalms. But it does assign Psalm 29 twice: every year on the Sunday celebrating the baptism of Jesus (1st Sunday after Epiphany) and again in Year B on Trinity Sunday. Therefore in churches that follow the lectionary, Psalm

29 is scheduled four times in three years. The Orthodox tradition places Psalm 29 at Epiphany when they celebrate Jesus' baptism.

Singing Psalm 29 Metrically

John Calvin turned to metrical settings of the psalms rather than singing them straight from Scripture as Luther preferred. Calvin held a high view of Scripture, but while exiled from Geneva, as pastor to French refuges in Strasbourg, he heard congregational singing of metrical psalms for the first time and immediately became convinced of the value of this form of psalmody. When he returned he succeeded in introducing metrical psalmody to a Protestant Geneva that had earlier embraced an iconoclastic rejection of all music in worship. Calvin's approach was based on his contemporary culture; sung metrical poetry was popular at the time. So in a radical decision he combined what Luther had kept separate: complete psalm texts re-written in the vernacular and in metrical form. Calvin was scrupulous about the responsibility of the poets. They had to accommodate rhythm and meter, so the texts would need to *add* words to the psalm, but the poet was not to *pad* the psalm by adding anything that was not there. Additions were only to exegete the psalm so as to make the meaning clear. This approach became the hallmark of the Reformed branch of the Reformation. Calvin's instincts were right; the Genevan Psalter was well received and immediately translated into several languages and sung to the same melodies in several countries.

A similar tradition sprang up simultaneously in England. The first metrical psalter was published in 1562, the same year as Calvin's Psalter. So there was widespread Protestant agreement as to a new way to sing the psalms congregationally. The Reformed tradition was even known for exclusive psalmody. On the continent Calvin opted for unison (no harmony), unaccompanied (no accompaniment), singing of only the psalms (no hymns) by the entire congregation (no choirs). In England harmony began earlier and hymns came earlier as well. A few small Reformed communities, especially from Dutch and Scottish communions, continue exclusive psalmody to this day; the Reformed Presbyterian Church in North America does permit harmony, but only unaccompanied metrical psalmody in worship with texts that follow the Scripture as literally as possible.

The great advantage of metrical psalmody is that people can sing the psalms to easily learned tunes. Some have spoken about borrowing tunes from secular sources, but most tunes sung in worship were composed specifically to be sung to psalms and hymns. Mentioning tunes is important because when the great period of hymn writing began in eighteenth century England, tunes that formerly were intended for psalms became associated with hymns, and eventually tunes composed specifically for hymns were set to metrical psalms.

Singing to easily learned tunes can become a disadvantage when a tune is distinctive enough to rival the text for attention. Chants by nature are not that memorable; their humble structures do not compete for attention since the text is what matters. Yet many tunes are very memorable and sometimes become primary so that the text becomes a vehicle for singing the tune rather than the other way around. Indeed, a good tune has saved many a mediocre text; however, a good text is not well served by a mediocre melody. The task of finding an appropriate melody that has a distinctive quality and yet does not compete with the text has been the challenge for every hymnal committee. The needed attention to poetic quality and appropriate melodies takes attention away from the psalm itself and in large measure accounts for the defense of chanted psalmody. In terms of texts, metrical psalmody stands between the chant tradition of singing the exact words of Scripture and the hymn tradition with poetry that may be quite loosely based on the psalms.

Now comes another issue: How do the unrhymed and unmetered Hebrew psalms fare when rewritten in meter and rhyme, the hallmarks of metrical poetry? Rather than the verse structure of Hebrew poetry that was preserved in chant, metrical psalmody groups verses into longer groups of lines in stanzas. The French poetry of Calvin's Genevan Psalter followed what was popular in both French and German poetry: lines of varying lengths and many different rhyme schemes and stanza lengths. Calvin's approach was to provide different structures to different types of psalms, for example, the short, bright lines for Psalm 47 (five syllables each), or the more reflective lines of Psalm 89 (12 or 13 syllables each). Each psalm was also given its own melody to preserve its distinctive character. When many psalms were sung each Sunday the practice of metrical psalmody took deep root and the common people learned many psalms by heart, aided by both rhyme and melody. In the Genevan Psalter, Psalm 29 is given eight lines, four of 7 syllables and four of 8 syllables with a very disciplined rhyme scheme of aa/bb/cc/dd, a rhyme scheme preserved also in many translations of this psalm set to the Genevan tune.

Over in England and Scotland, far fewer meters were used; in fact, one metrical structure was so common as to be called "Common Meter" with four lines of alternating 8 and 6 syllables in iambic meter (8.6.8.6, with unstressed followed by stressed syllables). This is the meter of the familiar psalm text by Isaac Watts, "O God Our Help in Ages Past," set to the well-known tune ST. ANNE (originally composed for Psalm 42). Other popular meters were named Short (6.6.8.6) and Long (8.8.8.8). Over the years the texts ranged from pedantic literalism with forced rhymes and awkward syntax to more graceful poetry that, however, sometimes moved beyond the biblical text or fell short of including the full imagery in the psalm. In the eighteenth century Isaac Watts wrote a complete collection of metrical psalm texts, but included New Testament concepts, arguing that we now sing as Christians. Therefore his Psalm 72 begins "Jesus shall reign." Most people think of these songs as hymns, not psalms, particularly since only part of the psalm setting is usually included. Watt's controversial approach split churches as he blurred the distinction between psalmody and hymnody. Nineteenth century metrical settings of the psalms downplayed many of the more earthy images in the psalms, following Victorian sensibilities. In the last forty years in the English-speaking world many excellent hymn writers have once more turned their gifts toward providing new metrical settings of the psalms in fresh contemporary English, people like Carl Daw, director of the Hymn Society in the United States and Canada, and John Bell, from the Iona Community of Scotland. Some metrical settings of the psalms have forsaken rhyme in order to recapture more closely the original Hebrew text. To get a glimpse of these differences of meter, rhyme, and vocabulary, here are five metrical examples from different centuries of the opening lines of Psalm 29:

> Give to the Lord, ye potentates, / give ye with one accord, all praise and honor, might and strength, / unto the living Lord.
> [Sternhold and Hopkins, 1562 (Iambic, Common Meter: 8.6. 8.6; 10 stanzas)]

> Give ye unto the Lord ye sons / that of the mighty be, all strength and glory to the Lord / with cheerfulness give ye.
> [Scottish Psalter, 1650 (Iambic, duple, Common Meter: 8.6. 8.6; 9 stanzas)]

> Give to the Lord, ye sons of fame, / give to the Lord renown and power, ascribe due honors to his name, / and his eternal might adore. [Isaac Watts, 1719 (Iambic, duple, Long Meter: 8.8. 8.8; 6 stanzas)]

> Now unto Jehovah, ye sons of the mighty / All glory and strength and dominion accord. Ascribe to him glory, and render him honor, / in beauty of holiness worship the Lord. [*Psalter* (Presbyterian), 1887 (Anapestic, triple, 12.11. 12.11; 4 stanzas)]

> Give glory to God, all you heavenly creatures; / all glory and power belong to the Lord! So drop to your knees and respect what is holy, be quiet and listen: the word of the Lord! [Calvin Seerveld, 1983 (Anapsetic, triple, 12.11 12.11; 5 stanzas)]

The first two examples could be sung to any number of Common Meter melodies and the final two were both set to the same tune (ARLES) in different generations of North American Psalters. The first four are rhymed; Watts even includes internal rhyme. Seerveld used repetition rather than rhyme. The first two examples cover only verse one and the others cover the first two verses. The same structure that began the psalm then follows through the longer center section of the psalm that describes the storm as well as the closing two verses that are so different in tone from the stormy center.

One of the distinctive features of Psalm 29 is the repetition of "Lord": four times in the opening and closing sections and ten times in the middle section with the added seven-fold repetition of "The voice of the Lord." To honor "the voice of the Lord," as it is rendered in most English translations, the final two examples chose triple meter; duple versions cannot easily use that expression. In fact, before the eighteenth century the triple anapestic meter was not considered to be "sufficiently respectable for church use," since it was also used for a "Tripping ballad form" and for satirical poetry (Lovelace, 76). Watts includes the word "Lord" five times and "voice" only twice, opting for varied expressions like "The Lord proclaims," "his voice divides," and "he speaks." The Hebrew hammering of "the voice of the Lord" throughout the middle section is lost in most metrical versions. Similarly, the word "glory" is key to the psalm, found four times with the final appearance as the climax in verse 9 when, at the end of describing God's power in the storm, all say "Glory!" But few metrical settings give the word "glory" climatic treatment.

One unrhymed attempt by Dale A. Schoening in his collection *Sing the Psalms* does honor the structure of Psalm 29 very well, set in five stanzas in 10.10.11.11, again in anapestic meter, with the suggested tune LYONS (or HANOVER, both known to "O Worship the King"). The center three stanzas open with "The voice of the Lord" and stanza 4 ends with the exact scriptural quote: "And all in his temple cry 'Glory.'" It is much easier to render Scripture faithfully when forgoing rhyme, but more difficult to provide aesthetically pleasing poetry.

The unrhymed setting in *Sing Glory* by Michael Perry to a tune composed for it by Norman Warren is wonderfully dramatic with a choral version even including echoes that remind one of echoing claps of thunder. It includes only the dramatic center section of the psalm with each of the three stanzas ending with "Glory, glory, glory!" But it only includes the word "voice" once:

> The God of heaven thunders, whose voice in cadent echoes
> resounds above the waters, and all the world sings, "Glory, glory, glory!"
>
> The desert writhes in tempest, wind whips the trees to fury,
> the lightning splits the forest, and flame diffuses Glory, glory, glory!
>
> The mighty God eternal is to the throne ascended,
> and we who are God's people within these walls cry, "Glory, glory, glory!"[1]

In sum, the great advantage of metrical poetry is that the psalms can be set to easily learned and memorable melodies. But there are many disadvantages as well: meter rules, the texts require adaptation that does not honor different or changing structures of given psalms, and all too often the tune is less a humble servant of the text than an equal if not dominant partner. Many congregations learn the psalms to a limited number of familiar melodies, often with associations with hymns, in a similar way that those who chant the psalms learn only a few psalm tones. Many congregations today are not interested in sing-

---

1. ©1973 The Jubilate Group (admin. by Hope Publishing Company, Carol Stream, Illinois 601881). All rights reserved. Used by Permission.

ing more than three or four stanzas, so psalm settings are either greatly condensed or congregations pick and choose sections of the psalms to sing, further aligning them with the hymn tradition rather than with psalmody.

Singing Psalm 29 Responsorially

When the Second Vatican Council introduced liturgical reforms in the Constitution of the Sacred Liturgy (*Sacrosanctum Concilium*) in 1963, one of the most significant was to involve all the people in "full, conscious, active" participation in worship, including communal singing of the psalms. The challenge for the Roman Catholic Church was to promote a type of psalmody that was pastorally sensitive while honoring the principles set forth by the Vatican Council, including the statement that "Gregorian chant . . . should be given pride of place in liturgical services" (*SC* 116). But the directive that "use of the Latin language is to be preserved in the Latin rites," was followed immediately by the statement that, "since the use of the mother tongue . . . frequently may be of great advantage to the people, the limits of its employment may be extended" (*SC* 36). The Vatican Council also encouraged the use of indigenous music around the world (*SC* 119). As Martin Luther and John Calvin had found four centuries earlier, the Roman Catholic Church found that singing in the language of the people caught on immediately worldwide. Gregorian chant quickly started disappearing, to the shock and deep sense of loss by those who loved that heritage. The Catholic Church was not prepared for the swift change to the vernacular and the corresponding need for new music. Into the vacuum created by the loss of Latin, much new music of varying quality was introduced. Since then the practice of psalmody has matured greatly and settled into especially one major approach, an approach that has also greatly influenced worship in Protestant churches: responsorial psalmody.

The Roman Catholic Church bypassed the metrical approach in favor of keeping the psalm texts intact and honored the long tradition of chanting the psalms by trained choirs or cantors. But, unlike Lutherans, the people were not asked to chant the psalms. The responsorial approach chose a new way to honor the principle of involving "the whole body of the faithful" in order that they "may be able to contribute that active participation which is rightly theirs" (*SC* 114).

The psalms were usually divided into sections with the assembly singing short memorable antiphons or refrains that highlight a particular aspect of the psalm. This Catholic approach of short refrains coincided with the rise of other short forms, like Taizé choruses and praise choruses that similarly had short repeated texts often based on a verse of a psalm. The rise in popularity of short forms, rather than the longer and richer texts of the metrical tradition of psalms and hymns, found ready acceptance across widely different liturgical traditions, including the charismatic movement and the growing youth culture for which music is extremely important.

Many Roman Catholic composers developed a rather distinctive and accessible way of writing in what has become known as "folk liturgical" style: the psalm settings of Marty Haugen, for example, fall into this category with settings for choir on the psalm texts and the assembly joining on a refrain. Many published anthem-like settings also include varied music for the different sections of the psalm so that the musical setting of the text is not all treated the same throughout the psalm. Choirs or cantors are required for these varied settings; when included in hymnals only the text of the psalm, not the music, is usually included because of the extra room needed for a longer composition.

The responsorial approach has also become widely accepted among mainline Protestant denominations that closely followed the reforms of Vatican II. Many Protestant choirs now take a more liturgical role in singing psalm texts together with congregational refrains rather than their all too common role of interjecting anthems into the liturgy. For Protestants without choirs the practice of creating refrains by extracting initial phrases from familiar hymns became a comfortable way to introduce psalmody to churches for which psalmody was quite new. Refrains in *Sing! A New Creation* include originally composed and hymn extracts, as well as Taizé melodies and phrases from praise choruses and global songs. There is much musical creativity and variety surrounding the composition and selection of music for psalm refrains.

When it comes to the text the challenge is to decide what short text the congregation will sing. In refrains built from hymns sometimes the congregation does not even sing a line from the psalm, but a line from a hymn that resonates with the psalm. For example, the first phrase of "What Wondrous Love Is This, O my Soul" was set to Psalm 22 in *Sing! A New Creation*. The choice is best taken on liturgical grounds, depending on its placement in the service or the emphasis taken in the sermon. Though the psalm itself is sung or read, the refrain emphasizes a particular slant and is what the people will remember.

For Psalm 29 there are numerous options. A refrain by Gary Chamberlain emphasizes the glory and power of God in the center of the psalm: "In splendor and power God's glory appears." Another by Steven Warner stresses the quieter prayer for peace at the close of the psalm: "Lord, bless your people with peace, the gift of your peace." A refrain by Geoffrey Boulton Smith combines those concepts in a single refrain: "Give strength to your people, Lord, and bless your people with peace." The *United Methodist Hymnal* uses a line from one of Charles Wesley's hymns: "With joy the Lord of Hosts proclaim; extol the great almighty name," set to the final two phrases of DUKE STREET (known to "Jesus Shall Reign").

The strength and advantage of the responsorial tradition are the accessibility of short refrains along with retaining the psalm text whether sung or read. The antiphons are short enough to be learned by rote and the repetition would encourage the people to offer the psalms as their own prayers in their own voices. This structure is embedded within Psalm 136, for example, with the main text of the psalm reserved for the choir of Levites and all the people responding with the refrain, "for his steadfast love endures forever." But for responsorial psalmody that same approach is extended to the entire psalter whether or not the original Hebrew structure included a refrain. So once more, one approach is applied to all the psalms even though few psalms exhibit a refrain structure. Another disadvantage is the sheer proliferation of psalm refrains, some directly taken from the psalm, some from hymns, some newly created. The brevity of refrains has encouraged many amateurs who write for their own congregations and, in fact, encouraged some of them to seek training in composition. But few amateurs or even published composers can match the depth and beauty of the short gems of composition like those of Jacques Berthier who composed most of the music for the Community of Taizé.

Conclusion

Given the three main traditions of chanting the psalms, singing the psalms reshaped into metrical poetry, and the varied possibilities in the more recent responsorial approach, how should Psalm 29 be sung? For the past four centuries most Western congregations depended on print; they were limited to what was included in their psalters and hymnals. But with technology now making it possible to project or copy new settings, congregations have access to much more.

Here are three concluding thoughts and questions. First, the starting point of choosing a particular setting of Psalm 29, as with any psalm, should be with the structure of the psalm itself. What are its main features that should be highlighted in a musical setting? What setting best honors the structure of the psalm? Second comes the liturgical question: where does the psalm best fit in the structure of the whole service so that this part of God's word is offered in prayer, in praise, or in lament, or whatever other context honors both the psalm and the liturgy.

A final question is an ecumenical one: considering the wide-spread renewal of psalmody, is there a way singing the psalms can help heal divisions in the church? The psalms are shared by us all. Only a few psalm settings from the metrical tradition have become known around the world, with Watt's setting of the first section of Psalm 90, "O God, Our Help in Ages Past," probably the most widely known. How welcome it would be for at least some psalm settings in the twenty-first century to become so well known that Christians would sing them everywhere, so that a melody would bring to mind the words of Scripture. To that end poets and composers, church musicians, worship planners and people in the pews together have a common calling: to "ascribe to the Lord glory and strength" (Psalm 29:1), and to pray that "the Lord give strength to his people" (v. 11), also in praying psalms returning this great gift from God back to God in worship.

Hymnals and Psalters Mentioned

Baughan, Michael, editor. *Sing Glory: Hymns, Psalms and Songs for a New Century.* Suffolk: Mayhew, 1999.

Brink, Emily R., editor. *Sing! A New Creation.* Grand Rapids: Calvin Institute of Christian Worship, Faith Alive Christian Resources, Reformed Church Press, 2001.

Evangelical Lutheran Worship. Minneapolis: Augsburg Fortress, 2006.

Schoening, Dale A. *Sing the Psalms: Metrical Psalm Settings Based on the Lectionary.* Lima, OH: Fairway, 1988.

Young, Carlton R. *United Methodist Hymnal.* Nashville: United Methodist Publishing House, 1989.

Books and Articles

Brink, Emily R. "Metrical Psalmody: A Tale of Two Traditions." *RefLitM* 23 (Winter 1989) 3–8.

———, and John D. Witvliet. "Contemporary Developments in Music in Reformed Churches Worldwide." In *Christian Worship in Reformed Churches Past and Present*, edited by Lukas Vischer, 324–47. Grand Rapids: Eerdmans, 2003.

The Liturgy Documents: A Parish Resource. Chicago: Liturgical, 1980.

Lovelace, Austin C. *The Anatomy of Hymnody.* Chicago: GIA Publications, 1965.

Proulx, Richard, and Raymond F. Golver. "Contemporary Use of Chant." In *The Hymnal 1982 Companion*, edited by Raymond F. Glover, 253–65. New York: The Church Hymnal Corporation, 1990.

Stapert, Calvin. *A New Song for an Old World: Musical Thought in the Early Church.* Grand Rapids: Eerdmans, 2007.

Witvliet, John D. *The Biblical Psalms in Christian Worship: A Brief Introduction and Guide to Resources.* Grand Rapids: Eerdmans, 2007.

10

Gods of Glory Ought to Thunder

The Canaanite Matrix of Psalm 29

Dennis Pardee *and* Nancy Pardee

STUDENTS OF THE HEBREW BIBLE QUICKLY BECOME AWARE OF THE conflicts between Yahwism and other religious systems in the formative period of Israelite/Jewish religion. In Palestine the Israelites were in close contact with other peoples whose religious beliefs and practices continuously vied for, and apparently frequently won, Israelite hearts and minds. Although the religious practices of the "Canaanites," the term of identification used for these neighboring peoples, were quite similar to those of the Israelites, for example in the emphasis on animal sacrifice and the use of song and prayer, the Canaanite religion was polytheistic and the representation of these gods in various material forms was considered normal. This was, of course, in stark contrast to Israelite religion which was, at an early stage, henotheistic (the worship of only one god among the many that were believed to exist) then monotheistic and which prohibited any physical representation of the deity. In no uncertain terms, the first of the Ten Commandments prohibits the worship of gods other than Yahweh while the second forbids the crafting of divine images.

> I am the Lord your God, who brought you out of the land of Egypt, out of the house of slavery; you shall have no other gods before me. You shall not make for yourself an idol in the form of anything that is in heaven above, or that is on the earth beneath or that is in the water under the earth. You shall not bow down to them or worship them for I the Lord your God, am a jealous God, punishing children for the iniquity of parents, to the third and fourth generation of those who reject me, but show-

ing steadfast love to the thousandth generation of those who love me and keep my commandments. (Exod 20:2–6)

What is actually known about Canaanite religion? Within the Bible itself one finds references, albeit negative ones, to Canaanite deities, in particular to the god Baal. For example, when the Israelite tribes encountered difficulty during the conquest of Canaan, the book of Judges states:

> ... the Israelites did what was evil in the sight of the Lord and worshipped the Baals; and they abandoned the Lord, the God of their ancestors, who had brought them out of the land of Egypt; they followed other gods from among the gods of the peoples who were all around them, and bowed down to them; and they provoked the Lord to anger. They abandoned the Lord, and worshiped Baal and the Astartes. So the anger of the Lord was kindled against Israel, and he gave them over to plunderers who plundered them, and he sold them into the power of their enemies all around, so that they could no longer withstand their enemies. (Judg 2:11–14)

Within the West Semitic languages, which include the Canaanite dialects of Hebrew and Phoenician as well as the Amorite dialects (peoples north and east of Canaan), "baal" has the meaning of "lord" and in that sense can be applied to human or divine beings. Thus in Hebrew it is found with the meaning "master" or "husband" on the one hand, or in reference to Canaanite gods on the other. As in the passage from Judges above, the latter use can sometimes occur in the singular as a proper name (often in connection with a place name), other times in the plural, where it is thought to denote either the Canaanite gods in general or the one god Baal in all his various geographical manifestations.

Elsewhere in the Bible prophets warn of the dire consequences that will befall the Israelites should they fail to reject the worship of the Canaanite gods and return wholeheartedly to the worship of Yahweh. The following warning appears in the book of the prophet Hosea:

> When Ephraim spoke, there was trembling; he was exalted in Israel; but he incurred guilt through Baal and died. And now they keep on sinning and make a cast image for themselves, idols of silver made according to their understanding, all of them the work of artisans. "Sacrifice to these," they say. People are kissing calves! Therefore they shall be like the morning mist

or like the dew that goes away early, like chaff that swirls from
the threshing floor or like smoke from a window. (Hos 13:1–3)

Moreover it was to such practices, abetted by several of the kings of Israel and Judah, that the Deuteronomistic History attributes the disasters that overtook the Northern Kingdom in the eighth and the Southern Kingdom in the sixth centuries BCE.

> They rejected all the commandments of the Lord their God and made for themselves cast images of two calves; they made a sacred pole, worshiped all the host of heaven, and served Baal. They made their sons and their daughters pass through fire; they used divination and augury; and they sold themselves to do evil in the sight of the Lord, provoking him to anger. Therefore the Lord was very angry with Israel and removed them out of his sight; none was left but the tribe of Judah alone. Judah also did not keep the commandments of the Lord their God but walked in the customs that Israel had introduced. The Lord rejected all the descendants of Israel; he punished them and gave them into the hand of plunderers, until he had banished them from his presence. (2 Kgs 17:16–20)

Although some of the people of Judah would eventually return to their land and rebuild, the Northern Kingdom as a political entity was lost forever.

But aside from this superficial and certainly one-sided description of the Canaanite religious systems found in the Bible, extra-biblical sources were scarce until the archaeological discovery in the modern era of documents from biblical times. In 1929, for example, the initial excavation of a Syrian tell (a large mound of earth hiding beneath its surface the remains of one or more layers of ancient settlements) situated approximately one-half mile inland from the northeastern shore of the Mediterranean, revealed something that would prove to be enormously illuminating for the study of the ancient Near East and in particular for students of the Hebrew Scriptures: the lost city-state of Ugarit. Located almost directly across from the northeast tip of Cyprus at the harbor called in Arabic Minet el-Beida ("white harbor"), ancient Ugarit, corresponding to the tell today known as Ras Shamra, had been mentioned in a fourteenth-century BCE administrative letter originating in Canaan but recovered from its destination at the site of el-Amarna in Egypt. But the discovery by a peasant of an ancient tomb within the Minet el-Beida harbor district in 1928 had drawn the attention of archaeologists, who, after beginning their work at this port site, soon transferred their attention to the nearby tell of Ras Shamra. The excavation of the port site was entrusted to the French scholar Claude Schaeffer, who, in the spring of 1929, began excavating the highest part of the tell (the "acropolis") and almost immediately and quite fortuitously happened upon a cache of inscribed clay tablets that soon disclosed the identity of the people who had once inhabited the site.

The tell itself measures about 3,300 feet at its greatest extent along the east-west axis and about 1,650 feet north-south; the north side of the tell has been badly eroded by the flood waters of a stream that flows there. The excavations have revealed multiple periods of occupation dating back to the seventh millennium BCE. The remains of a settlement identifiable with the city known as Ugarit are found in two stages: the first from about 2100–1600 BCE and the second from 1500–1185 BCE. The archaeological trail ends in the early twelfth century when the city was burned and destroyed, presumably by the Sea Peoples, invaders from the west that included the infamous Philistines, well known from the historical books of the Bible. During the final stage, however, the kingdom had been prosperous and internationally renowned (though generally as a vassal state of a more powerful neighbor), with buildings that included among them two temples (built during the previous Middle Bronze Age) and a prominent palace.

As if this were not enough to pique the interest of the archaeologists, anthropologists, sociologists, historians, and numerous other scholars who study the ancient Near East, many of the tablets recovered there were written in a previously unknown cuneiform script. Cuneiform is the representation of language by means of configurations of wedge shapes impressed into soft clay using a stylus with a square tip. This method of writing had long been used to write Akkadian, a member of the wider Semitic language family and the lingua franca of the period (a lingua franca is a language used broadly among different peoples for the purpose of business and administration, much as English is today). But the wedge configurations in Akkadian represented syllables and a minimum of 200 different signs would have been in the repertory of any practicing scribe. The newly discovered Ugaritic script had a mere thirty signs, indicating an alphabetic character, that is, each sign represented one consonantal sound. The alphabetic method of representing language had developed in Syro-Palestine in the first part of the second millennium BCE and is the source of our current Roman alphabet. This newly discovered Ugaritic language combined the ease of an alphabetic system with the cuneiform method of text production. In addition, the length and form of the words indicated that Ugaritic was also a Semitic language and, once it was deciphered, it was clear that is was an earlier relative of Biblical Hebrew.

The number of texts found at Ras Shamra is now well over four thousand, a sizeable archive in absolute terms and the only one of its kind from coastal Palestine/Syria. In terms of actual material recovered, the languages represented are primarily Akkadian and Ugaritic, though there are also remains of texts representing other language-families of the time, such as Hurrian, Egyptian and Hittite. The genres attested include letters, administrative texts, and, most impressively, several lengthy mythological texts. All of these were important to scholars of the Hebrew Scriptures in that they provided historical evidence from a culture related to that of the Canaanites as we know them from the Bible. Though the city-state of Ugarit is to be classified as Amorite and not Canaanite, both groups are part of the larger West Semitic culture.

In addition, the Ugaritic texts, likely dating from about the mid-thirteenth century BCE until the end of the kingdom in the early twelfth century, offered abundant new material for charting the linguistic development of Biblical Hebrew prior to the stages represented in the Hebrew Scriptures. They also demonstrated that the method of creating poetic texts that is found in the Hebrew Bible, that is, via parallel verses of two or three segments (bicola and tricola) of roughly similar length, was also shared by both languages and indeed by the Northwest Semitic languages overall. Even more astonishing, however, was the fact that the mythological texts of Ugarit included stories of the god Baal.

From these texts it is learned that Baal is a god of rainstorms and hence of vegetal fertility in general. Historically "Baal" with the meaning "lord" was an epithet applied to the inland Syrian weather deity Haddu (or Hadad) that came subsequently to be used as a divine name in its own right. Although Baal was named in earlier texts, the new documents from Ugarit now provided a plethora of details allowing for a reconstruction of his characteristics and his place within the Amorite-Canaanite pantheon. One of the great gods of Ugarit, second in rank only to El, the head of the pantheon, Baal was also denoted by the epithets "Prince," "Mighty," and "Cloud-Rider." Ugaritic made clear that the various Baals mentioned in the Bible were local manifestations of one and the same god. In the Ugaritic texts Baal is a times identified as the son of Dagan, but is at the same time also under the authority of El.

The rain provided by Baal through the windows of his palace (openings in the clouds) high up on Mt. Saphon (the highest mountain in Syria, about 40 km north of Ugarit) was often accompanied by his mighty weapons, thunder and lightning, a fact that is portrayed on an ancient stele found at Ugarit where the god holds a club in his right hand and what appears to be a lightning bolt in the other, the latter in the form of a spear with vegetation sprouting from its handle, a clear representation of the life-giving function of the showers for which Baal was responsible. In the text from Ugarit where Baal's conflict and subsequent defeat of the divine Sea/River (Ugaritic Yammu/Naharu, cognate with the Hebrew common nouns "yam" and "nahar") are recounted, the artisan deity Kothar-and-Hasis provides Baal with two weapons, a mace and a type of sword, representative of thunder and lightning.

Indeed, it is the story of Baal's defeat of Sea/River with which the "Baal Cycle" from Ugarit begins. Elsewhere in the Ugaritic texts and probably belonging to another mythological stratum there is reference to a similar conflict with the sea monsters Lotan and Tunnan (known in the Hebrew Bible as "Leviathan" and "Tannin"). The defeat of Sea/River is followed by the account of the construction of a palace for Baal signifying his kingship in place of Yammu, and finally that of his death when he is ordered into the underworld by the god Mot ("Death," cognate with Hebrew *mot*). Mot's subsequent defeat by Baal's angry sister/consort Anatu, however, allows Baal to return to life and this sequence is generally believed to reflect the yearly agricultural cycle, that is, the dearth of rain in summer and the return of the storms in fall.

The presentation of Baal in the Hebrew Bible is not without ambiguity. On the one hand, Baal is denigrated and his worship prohibited; on the other hand, the characteristics of Baal are reassigned to Yahweh, as in the following passages:

> Yet God my King is from old,
> working salvation in the earth.
> You divided the sea by your might,
> You broke the heads of the dragons in the waters.
> You crushed the heads of Leviathan;
> You gave him as food for the creatures of the wilderness.
> (Ps 74:12–14)

> On that day the Lord with his cruel and great and strong sword will punish Leviathan the fleeing serpent, Leviathan the twisting serpent, and he will kill the dragon that is in the sea. (Isa 27:1)

Like Baal, Yahweh is "king" and in Psalm 48 Yahweh's presence on Mount Zion, the location of the Temple of Jerusalem, is paralleled with Mount Zaphon (Saphon), the home of Baal.

> Great is Yahweh and highly praised in the city of our God,
> the holy mountain, fairest of heights, the joy of all the earth,
> Mount Zion, the heights of Zaphon, the city of the great king.
> (Ps 48:1–2, author's translation)

Moreover, Yahweh is also portrayed as appropriating the clouds for his chariot:

> He it is who raises his palace upon the waters,
> makes the clouds his chariot,
> travels on the wings of the wind. (Ps 104:3, author's translation)

Beyond the simple appropriation of one or two individual characteristics of Baal to Yahweh, however, Psalm 29 seems to reflect a familiarity with a significant portion of the Baal story as we know it from the Ugaritic texts. While some scholars would go so far as to see an actual Canaanite hymn behind the words of Psalm 29, a more likely scenario envisions a Hebrew author who knows the myths and who wants to use their phraseology to emphasize the superiority of Yahweh. Compare Psalm 29 to the following section from the Baal Cycle on the building of the palace of Baal.

> Mighty Baal speaks up:
> "I believe I'll charge Kothar this very day,
> Yea, Kothar, this very moment,
> With opening a window in (my) house,
> A latticed window in (my) palace;
> And I'll open up the rift of the clouds."

> On account of Kothar-and-Hasis' (previous) speech,
> Kothar-and-Hasis begins laughing,
> Lifting up his voice and crying out:
> "Did I not say to you, O Mighty Baal,
> 'You'll come around, O Baal, to my word'?"
> He opens a window in the house,
> A latticed window in the palace;
> Baal opens up a rift of the clouds.
> His holy voice Baal gives forth repeatedly,
> Repeatedly pronounces, does Baal, the outpouring of his lips.
> His holy voice causes the earth to tremble,
> At the outpouring of his lips, the mountains take fright.
> [*damaged line*]
> the high places of the earth totter.
> Baal's enemies grasp the trees,
> Haddu's adversaries (grasp) the slopes of the mountain.
> Mighty Baal speaks up:
> "O enemies of Baal, why have you taken fright?
> Why have you taken fright, you who arm yourselves against Dimaranu?
> Does not Baal sight where his hand (will strike),
> (when) the *kittugaddu* of cedar (is) in his right hand?
> With Baal enthroned at his house,
> What person, king or commoner,
> Can set up his own dominion in the earth?
> So why don't I send a courier
> To Mot, son of El,
> A messenger to the beloved lad of El?
> Let Mot cry out (all he wants) from his throat,
> Let the beloved one repeat from his very innards,
> 'I alone am the one who rules over the gods,
> who fattens gods and men,
> who sates the hordes of the earth.'" (RS2.[008] + VII 14–52)[1]

The echoes of the portrayal of Baal in this text from Ugarit in the description of Yahweh in Psalm 29 are unmistakable. First and foremost, both gods are associated with the phenomenon of rain. The "voice" of Baal, that is, thunder, comes out of the clouds with the result that the earth "trembles" (line 31), the "mountains take fright" (line 32), "the high places of the earth totter," (lines 34–35), his "enemies grasp the trees," his

---

1. Ugaritic texts cited here by excavation number. For other text reference systems see Dietrich, et al.

"adversaries the slopes of the mountains" (lines 35–37). In similar fashion the "voice" of Yahweh "has broken the cedars of Lebanon" (Ps 29:5), has caused Mounts Lebanon and Siryon "to dance like a calf . . . like a young bovid" (Ps 29:6), has caused "the steppe of Qadesh" as well as the "hinds" to "writhe" (Ps 29:8–9). Day, in fact, believes the seven references to this voice/thunder of Yahweh in Psalm 29 to be the equivalent to the "seven lightning's . . . eight storehouses of thunder" of Baal found in RS 24.245.3–4 (Day, 548–49). Just as Baal used lightning to create rifts in the clouds (lines 18, 23) through which his voice/thunder (lines 29–32) and lightning (lines 40-41) reach the earth, so Yahweh "splits off flames of fire" (Ps 29:7) that "stripped bare the forests" (Ps 29:9). Moreover, like "Mighty Baal" who sits "enthroned at his house" (line 42) and mockingly asserts that it is he and not Mot who "fattens gods and men" and "sates the hordes of the earth" (lines 50–52), so Yahweh "has taken his seat (on the throne) king of all time" (Ps 29:10), he "constantly gives strength to his people" and "constantly blesses his people with well-being" (Ps 29:11).

Added to the significance of the number of images shared by the two texts is the parallelism seen in their order of occurrence indicating that both likely stem from a commonly known mythology: the deity's status and power are connected with his dwelling; from this dwelling the god makes its proclamations, that is, issues forth thunder and lightning, which shake the earth and create fear among his inhabitants; these phenomena, however, guarantee that the god is king and that it is through him that all of existence is blessed. On the other hand, the reference to the "voice" of Yahweh being "over the waters" in verse 3 and as in some way ruling over the Great Flood in verse 10 certainly picks up the theme of Baal's defeat of Sea/River from earlier in the Ugaritic text. If one might stretch a bit to see in the title given to Yahweh in verse 10, "king of all time," an allusion to his ruling also over the dead, it could be said that Psalm 29 presents what might be termed an epitome of all three portions of the Baal Cycle.

Still it is clear from Psalm 29 that, for the Israelites, it is the Lord who is to be worshiped above all other deities, in fact all heavenly beings ("sons of the gods") worship and praise Yahweh (Ps 29:1). Thus the use of the themes and motifs found in Baal tradition by the author of Psalm 29 seem intentionally designed to show the superiority of Yahweh over his Canaanite competitor. The author is both persuading his fellow Israelites of the wisdom of placing their allegiance in the Lord and warning them of its necessity, even in the face of the temptation to turn to or accommodate the worship of Baal.

Where might one find a context for the creation of such a poem? If one takes as genuine the conflict with Canaanite religion as well as the archaic features of the text, a potential location might be in the place and time of the prophet Hosea, that is the Northern Kingdom of the eighth century BCE. Day, for example, sees in Hosea evidence of what the prophet considered to be a dangerous syncretism between Yahweh and Baal on the part of some of his audience. In a hopeful prediction of a return of the people to the true worship of Yahweh, the prophet states, "On that day, says the Lord, you will call me, 'My husband,' and no longer will you call me, 'My Baal'" (Hos 2:16). Day further sees in the motif of the harlot wife in the book of Hosea the existence of sacred prostitution in the Baal cult, a theme seen elsewhere in the Hebrew Bible though it must be noted that this is nowhere mentioned in the Ugaritic texts. Lastly it may be that the theme of death, resurrection, and subsequent fertility found in Hosea 5:12—6:3 and chapters 13–14 is reminiscent of the mythic conflict between Baal and Mot (Day, 548–49).

Finally, it must be noted that the Baal tradition appropriated in Psalm 29 appears to continue its metamorphosis in Psalm 96, likely an updated version of the earlier psalm. Here the "sons of gods" have become the "tribes of the people" (Ps 96:7), indeed there are no other gods, only "shams" (Ps 96:5). And Yahweh no longer thunders and rules over the waters, on the contrary, it is the sea itself that "thunders" Yahweh's praise (Ps 96:11). Nor is it simply Israel who benefits from the blessings of the Lord, but it is all the nations. This is, indeed a "new song," making use of the motifs of an old song to proclaim a new era brought about by Yahweh's salvific acts.

Bibliography

Day, John. "Baal." In *ABD* 1:545–49.
Dietrich, Manfried, et al. *The Cuneiform Alphabetic Texts from Ugarit, Ras Ibn Hani and Other Places (KTU: Second, Enlarged Edition)*. ALASP 8. Münster: Ugarit-Verlag, 1995.
Pardee, Dennis. "The Baalu Myth (1.86)." In *Canonical Compositions from the Biblical World*, edited by William W. Hallo and K. Lawson Younger Jr., 241–74. COS 1. Leiden: Brill, 1997.

———. "Canaan." In *The Blackwell Companion to the Hebrew Bible*, edited by Leo G. Perdue, 151–68. Oxford: Blackwell, 2001.

———. "On Psalm 29: Structure and Meaning." In *The Book of Psalms: Composition and Reception*, edited by Peter W. Flint and Patrick D. Miller, Jr., 153–83. VTSup 99. Leiden: Brill, 2005.

Watson, W. G. E., and Nicolas Wyatt. *Handbook of Ugaritic Studies*. HO 1.39. Leiden: Brill, 1999.

Wyatt, Nicolas. *Religious Texts from Ugarit: The Words of Illimilku and His Colleagues*. BibSem 53. Sheffield: Sheffield Academic, 2002.

Yon, Marguerite. *The City of Ugarit at Tell Ras Shamra*. Winona Lake, IN: Eisenbrauns, 2006.

11

Psalm 29 in African Indigenous Churches in Nigeria

David Tuesday Adamo

TO MY MIND, THE BOOK OF PSALMS PROVIDES THE MOST RELIABLE theological, pastoral, and liturgical resources in the biblical tradition. No wonder then that Psalms is referred to as the hymnal of the Second Temple. It provides the window through which ancient Israel's response to God's presence or absence may be viewed and has arguably been read more than any other book of the Bible. No doubt, the Bible is the most translated and the most read book.

Although it would seem that Psalms study in all its dimension has been lost, it is gratifying to see encouraging signs that an effort is being made to recover the Psalms, especially in African Christianity. In Africa, both biblical and non-biblical scholars are making the Psalter the focus of intensive research and discussion. New perspectives on the Psalter are coming up daily. Pastors, teachers, other Christians, and non-Christians are trying to rediscover the Psalter's invaluable resources, not only for their academic gratification, but also for their own spiritual lives and the spiritual development of their community.

The purpose of this chapter is to examine Psalm 29 in African Indigenous Churches and to discuss how African biblical scholars approach Psalms existentially. Most of the western scholars study the Psalms for the sake of scholarship, but Africans study Psalms in light of their culture and make use of them for daily existence. Just as General Booth, founder of the Salvation Army, believed that the devil should not have all the best tunes of this world and thus adapted the popular music of his day for the expression of the worship of God, so African

Christians adapt African popular culture in their worship and interpretation of Psalm 29.

Who are the African Indigenous Churches?

A brief survey of Nigerian African Indigenous Churches is appropriate. As a group these churches have been given many names. "Aladura Churches" (Praying Churches), so-called because of their emphasis on the power of prayer, are Yoruba in origin (*Ijo Aladura*). "Pentecostal Churches" is a western designation used because of the manner in which prayer and biblical interpretation occurs. "African Independent Churches" reflects their claim to be separated from western mainline denominational control; "Protest Churches" reflects the same independent status. The name "Zionist" is used to reflect a Pentecostal manner of praying and healing in the Spirit. Because of the white robes many wear, in what is believed to be the garb of the angels in heaven, some call them "White Garment Churches." The phrase "Ethiopian Churches" underscores the political nature of their establishment.

The formation of African Indigenous Churches [AIC] is the result of ecclesiastical experimentation with its origins faced with much opposition from the static mainline churches. The dynamic AIC adaptability to rapid social change can be seen in their liturgy, choruses, ritual innovations, emphasis on special methods of sharing, caring, healing, and economic concern in times of deprivation. Nonetheless, they still retain the basic worship pattern of the mainline churches from which they separated.

There are many churches in Nigeria, so many that almost every street has a church. It is important to understand the type of church AIC represents in Nigeria, but also to recognize that these churches are not limited to Nigeria or even to Africa, but exist all over the world. As representative of the AIC, I would like to discuss the histories of the following churches.

Christ Apostolic Church was founded in Nigeria by Joseph Ayo Babalola, a native of Odo Owa, Ilofa, and Kwara State, Nigeria. He was born in 1904 and attended Anglican Primary School in Osogbo, Osun State, Nigeria. He organized a prayer meeting and Bible study in the Anglican Church of his hometown, from which he was later excommunicated. He continued his missionary work in the house of a lay reader

Elder Olayemi, who was subsequently also excommunicated. In the face of such opposition Babalola left Odo Owa for Ibadan and Lagos, where he met Pastor Odubanjo, who in turn, introduced Babalola at a meeting in Ilesha as a man full of the Holy Spirit. One day Babalola raised a dead child who was on the way to the cemetery to be buried. While conducting a meeting at Benin, Edo State, he was arrested and jailed for six months. Because of Faith Tabernacle's persecution it was affiliated with an apostolic church in Bradford, Great Britain, as a way of seeking external assistance. The affiliation led to the adoption of the name Apostolic Church, British Apostolic missionaries visiting the churches in Nigeria, and personal contacts with the British government leading to the release of Babalola from prison. He then continued his work establishing Assemblies, schools and apostolic churches. With the growth of the church its name changed again to Christ Apostolic Church and it is by this name that it is known in Great Britain and the United States where most of its members are African immigrants or of African descent.

Cherubim and Seraphim Churches are among the most prominent AIC in Nigeria. They are very active and aggressive in the practice of their religion in a way that is indigenous to the people of Africa, particularly the Yoruba of Nigeria. Although there is a firm belief among members that the church was not founded by a human, there is historical evidence that it started as a prayer group in Lagos in 1925 under the leadership of Moses Orimolade Tunolase. The prophet Orimolade was born with a crippled leg in Ikare Akoko, Ondo State, Nigeria, in the 1870s. All of a sudden he had a vision to go to a stream to use its water for the purpose of healing; he obeyed and was partially healed. Soon after this miracle he became a traveling evangelist. Between 1916 and 1924 he traveled to many parts of Yoruba land and the Midwest of Nigeria. He continued his ministry without any objective of establishing a church until he met a teen-aged girl named Abiodun Akinsowon.

The Church of the Lord (Aladura) was founded by Oshitelu who was born at Ogere in 1902. He renounced his first two names at his baptism and took the name Josiah Oluwalowo. At a young age he was zealous for the Lord in the Anglican Church at Ogere. He said that he was warned to stop the use of traditional medicine, put his faith in God, read psalms for his daily devotion and fast. He followed the instructions of the Prophet Somoye and started praying and fasting; he claimed to have heard the voice of God confirming Somoye's prediction for him. As he continued in this spiritual development, he was noticed by some elders of the Anglican Church who warned him to desist from such unorthodox practices; when he refused he was excommunicated from the Anglican Church. In 1929 he emerged as a prophetic teacher organizing his first revival in his hometown on June ninth and inaugurated his church in July of 1930 at Ogere. His fame spread quickly and the Faith Tabernacle Church became interested in his evangelistic ministry, but his use of strange names and his so-called "sealed words," separated them. Prophet Shield claimed that, in accordance with Ezekiel 33:7, special names of God were revealed to him: *AWOBISLILLAL* (healer), *ARRABABLALHUS*, and *ANOMOLNOMOLLAHHUJAH*. The church and the disciples embarked on mass evangelistic campaigns leading to expansion in the towns of Oyo and Ijebu, Ondo, and Ekiti. The very gifted evangelist, Mr. Adeleke Adejobi, also joined the church and became Oshitelu's disciple. In 1940 this able evangelist opened a church in Lagos. In 1945, in response to a vision to expand the church beyond Nigeria, Oshitelu commissioned Apostles Adejobi and Oduwole, who established the church in Sierra Leone and Liberia respectively. The church has since spread to Ghana, other African countries, Glasgow and the United States.

Celestial Church of Christ (CCC) is one of the most attractive and flourishing indigenous churches in Africa today. It was established in 1947 by Samuel Bilewu (Bileou) Joseph Oshoffa, who was born on May 18, 1909, in a small village near Port-Novo, Dahomey (Benin). During his infancy his father arranged for him to live with Methodist Bishop David Hodonu Loco. Oshoffa attended a Methodist Primary School but was not allowed to attend seminary because he refused to mold bricks for their hostels. As a result he was forced to learn carpentry, his father's profession. In May, 1947, he was lost in the forest for three months living on honey and water while engaged in fervent prayer. When he came out of the forest he had a revelation in which God appointed him as a worldwide evangelist to preach the Gospel of Jesus Christ. As part of the assurance of this call he healed a young man by laying his hands on the dead body. As a result of this miracle many people came to Oshoffa's house where the man resided. Pastor Oshoffa performed many more miracles that baffled the people. At Porto Novo he healed and brought back to life his nephew among many others. Confirmation of his call came on September 29, 1947, when a vision of a ray of light and an angel assured him of his ministry; a member of his praying band fell into a trance affirming his vision. After this Oshoffa heard God's voice telling him the type of church he should establish. One of his members, in a trance, received a message: "Eglise du Christianisme Celeste" (Yoruba: "Ijo mimo ti ti Kkristi lat Orun wa"), meaning "Holy Assembly of Christ from Heaven." This was the beginning of the identification of the prayer group with the name Celestial Church of Christ.

Characteristics of African Indigenous Churches

These indigenous churches are uniform, sharing many characteristics. Of course, with few exceptions these characteristics are probably true of all AIC. The most prominent common characteristic is an *emphasis on African worldview*. In reading and interpreting the Bible this African worldview distinguishes African from western Christianity. The missionary/western ways of interpreting the Bible are too foreign to meet the urgent needs of Africans. AIC are down-to-earth in their belief, doctrine, and response to the problems of their African congregations. These churches preach the message that is rooted in African culture and in the light of the existence of evil spirits, witches and wizards, dreams, trances and visions. They respond to these problems through exorcism, rituals, sacrifices, prayers, fasting, bathing, and the power of words.

There is a strong and universal belief in *divine healing* among AIC. In Africa, where hospitals and orthodox medicine are beyond the reach of many Africans, one would expect that the promise of special healing by the Almighty God would attract visitors. In fact, the most pungent reason given for becoming members of AIC is *cura divina*. Special days (usually Wednesday and Friday) are set aside for healing purposes. There are series of testimonies about miracles that have been performed by God through these churches. Most of them claim that these healings take place after the failure of the hospitals and traditional healers. Most of those who are healed remain as members of these churches. Sometimes, spiritual or faith healing homes that serve as clinics are set up adjacent to the churches for the sick and pregnant women.

Prayer is also wide spread in all AIC throughout Africa. No wonder the Yoruba people of Nigeria refer to these churches as *Aladura* (praying people). The leaders are also referred to as prayer father (*Baba*

Aladura) and praying mother (*Iya Aladura*). There are always prayer groups called praying warriors (*A f'adura Jagun*-Yoruba, *Mpaec-Kuo*-Akan in Ghana). Their major responsibilities in the churches are to pray and fast for the needy, the sick, and special programs of the churches. Several places are designated for prayer, places such as mercy land, beaches, Garden, and others. They firmly believe that their prayers could be heard from these places more than from anywhere else. Most of them use special prayer aids such as candles, the book of Psalms, incense, palm fronds, and special books with the list of the holy names of God to be pronounced repeatedly.

There is an emphasis on *spirituality*. Many of these churches prefer to be called spiritual churches (*Ijo Emi* in Yoruba, *Sunsuni* in Akan, *Momo sulemo* in Ga, *Ishoshi rerhi* in Urhobo, *Uka onso* in Nsuko-Igbo). By this they claim to be filled and directed by the Holy Spirit in their activities. The purpose of establishment of the churches is always spiritual. Spiritual interpretation is given to all events, especially misfortunes such as sicknesses, unemployment, disappointments, poverty, and barrenness. Spiritual solutions are prescribed for these problems. That is why faith healing services and exorcism are constantly part of the activities of the church. The Holy Spirit is prominent as manifested in their interpretation of visions, dreams, ecstatic behavior, and prophetic utterances. The members are advised to wear white gowns because it is a sign of holiness and purity, which the Holy Spirit prefers.

There is an unusual enthusiasm for *evangelism and revival* among AIC. Most of their leaders are itinerary preachers who go from one place to another preaching revival. This was very true of Joseph Babalola, Moses Orimolade, Oshitelu, Oshoffa, and others all around Africa. Ordinary members are always advised to lead about seven to twenty revival or open-air revival crusades outside the church. This led to the rapid growth of their churches.

Africans are action-oriented people. They enjoy *flexible worship services* with demonstrative forms of worship rather than the dull Eurocentric liturgy of the mission churches. Everyone has an opportunity to participate in spirit and soul. AIC have made African participants feel more at home with chanting, clapping, singing, dancing and foot stamping. Most of the time such activity is absent in mainline missionary churches. Everyone is inspired to pray, to deliver a message, to sing and give testimonies. Most of the songs take the form of indigenous lyrics with invocations, spontaneous composition and responsorial type songs. The use of native musical instruments such as bells and drums are always attractive to both the members and non-members attending worship services.

The *elaborate role of women* is a distinctive characteristic of these churches. Unlike the mission churches that preach equality of sexes yet make men hold nearly all the principle positions of authority, AIC elevate women to *all* important ecclesiastical positions. It is not unusual to have prophetesses and deaconesses, Reverend Mothers, Lady Leaders, Mothers in Israel, Superior Mothers, Praying Mothers, lay evangelists, women church planters, and other leadership names in the AIC. In these churches women are more possessed, they prophesy, dance, sing, clap, give testimony more than do men. They are always in the majority and more active. In fact they are church founders.

One of the major characteristics of these churches is the *emphasis on the power of words* spoken by the prophets and apostles and those read and recited from the Bible. There is an emphasis on the memorization of the words of God and the repetitive pronunciation of certain words for effectiveness. Members are instructed to learn to say these words not only repeatedly, but also at certain times and certain places for their potency. The background of this practice is African culture and religion, where words are regarded as potent if repeated and said at certain times and places, mostly in the middle of the night. The word of God may be prescribed to be read seven times during midnight and while naked.

Like the African indigenous religion and culture, a strong belief in the *power in names* dominates these churches. They claim that special names of God are revealed to them to heal, to bring success in life and to protect against evil forces. Members are encouraged to repeat God's names as part of their prayers. Booklets containing the revealed names of God are printed for members and for the general public. There is no doubt whatsoever that those names are potent. Most of the names include names for God from the Hebrew Bible.

Africentric Interpretation of Psalm 29 by African Indigenous Churches

The history of psalm interpretation is certainly a history of constant change. In every age interpreters have found and focused on different dimensions of the literature of the Old Testament, calling for shifts in approach. It is quite important briefly to relate the history of such shifts. Africentric interpretation of Psalm 29 is not independent of Eurocentric Psalms traditions that form a background to AIC. Therefore Africentric interpreters do not condemn the Eurocentric interpretation. They both go hand in hand. This is true because most Africentric scholars are trained in the west and those not trained in the west are schooled in Eurocentric methods of interpretation.

The beginning of psalms studies considered the psalms as the handiwork of individual authors who composed songs and prayers for individual devotion, responding to their situation in life; one discerned the author and the particular situation. David became the decisive means of interpretation because he is considered to be the author of the book of Psalms, itself considered to be a collection of his songs, praise and piety. In the middle of the nineteenth century the historical critical scholars called into question the Davidic authorship of the psalms because of contradictions between the account of David's life in the book of Samuel and that of the psalms, not to mention the connection between some of the psalms and biblical literature from the period after David's life. These scholars examined psalms using historical critical methods rather than spiritual and theological methods, determining the psalms to be late documents.

The German scholar Hermann Gunkel saw the inadequacy of the historical-critical method. He postulated that psalms, rather than being the work of pious individual persons, were related to worship in ancient Israel. He started the classification of the psalms into forms and types, or genres (*Gattung*), and tried to determine their life setting in ancient Israel. Sigmund Mowinckel took the next step in Psalm interpretation by saying that the psalms represented the actual songs and prayers used in public worship in ancient Israel before the destruction of Jerusalem (587/586 BCE). This is referred to as the cult functional approach. The historical critical method, form critical, and cult functional approaches are not radically different from each other and became the influential approaches to studying Psalms through refinements and extensions to include many different settings. Scholars like James Muilenburg called for the need to supplement form-critical study with rhetorical and literary features of the psalms. Brevard Childs developed a canonical approach to the study of Psalms when he argued the need to go beyond a historical, cult functional and rhetorical approach to place more emphasis on the final form of the text of the Psalms (Childs, 378) and to understand that the book of Psalms is not just a collection of liturgical materials, but had the purpose of being read and heard. All of this western tradition comes to bear on Psalm 29.

Psalm 29 is a victory hymn which can be divided into three parts: 1) the call/summon to praise Yahweh (vv. 1-2); 2) praising Yahweh's voice (vv. 3-9); and 3) the praise of Yahweh in the temple (vv. 10-11). According to Walter Brueggemann's classification, Psalm 29 falls among the group of psalms denoted as "Psalm of New Orientation" and it is an enthronement psalm. It is a "psalm of new orientation" because it, along with Psalm 114, provides the basis for a new life and hope in "the governance of God" over the universe. The author therefore calls for a reenactment in worship of the true God. This is one of the most vivid, dramatic and ancient psalms in the Bible. Indeed, Psalm 29 has also been identified as originally having been a Canaanite/Phoenician psalm. Brueggemann considers this a Canaanite psalm that was taken over verbatim by Israel, save for inserting the name of Yahweh where the name of the Canaanite deity originally had appeared, because it reflects Canaanite mythology and rhetorical structures (142).

In Psalm 29 the psalmist "literally recreates the crash and reverberation, the rolling rumble and crackling explosion of the thunder and lightening" (Durham, 228). Seven times "the voice of the Lord" was mentioned. Such is the recognition of the power in the voice and the recitation of the words of the Lord. The psalmist finds more than a display of God's omnipotence, but his comfort, assurance and healing as well. The psalm is one of the most distinctive affirmations that God is both Lord of nature and its forces that was usually attributed to the god Baal by people living in Canaan (Craigie, 249). All the attributes usually attributed to Baal were transferred to Yahweh in this psalm with a vivid imagery of thunderstorm. The praise is not only for his power over nature but for his gift of victory, a gift given because of his strength. God who is sovereign in human affairs is also sovereign in the control over human environment and the world of nature. It is interesting that there is no explicit reference to this psalm in the New Testament even though this is one of the oldest psalms in the Bible. The language may have been the language of Canaanites, but it is still the original creation of a brilliant Hebrew poem as he sees God in storm and as God of nature (Durham, 228–29).

It is surprising that very few scholars ever think of attributing this psalm to African psalms despite the years of sojourn in Africa and the resemblance to Egyptian psalms. When full investigation is conducted on the songs of the African gods, especially Yoruba gods and goddesses (Ogun, Oya, Ifa, Orunmila, Obatala), scholars may be surprised at the result.

Those of us African biblical scholars trained in the west soon discovered upon returning to Africa that the very western methodological tradition in which we were schooled did not satisfy the need in Africa. The result of this is to find other satisfactory methods that will meet the need and the understanding of African people at home and abroad. This has to do with relating specific biblical issues to the situation in Africa. This method is different from the western methodology in that the particular focus is not only the historical and literary context of the passage read, but also African context. Although western critical tools and training are used, the context and the conclusion arrived at are always different from that of western scholarship. Unlike most western biblical scholars who labeled Psalm 29 as a hymn of victory and a declaration of Yahweh's omnipotence, African biblical scholars and ordinary readers consider it a psalm of "protection" and "defense, liberation, healing, and success" against enemies (Adamo, *Reading and Interpreting*, 49–108). Since this African interpretation of Psalm 29 is closely tied to the use of African culture and worldview, it is important to discuss at this stage the African concept of enemies and the African attitude to their enemies before the advent of Christianity.

The nature and process of dealing with enemies in African indigenous tradition is remarkably different from that of the western world. To indigenous Africans the presence of evil, witches, sorcerers, evil spirits and all kinds of enemies are painfully real. They believe that they are responsible for all the evil things that happen all over the world. In African tradition all relations, children and adult, are taught the existence and the activities of enemies. The need to be protected from them is taken seriously and animate and inanimate items such as stones, sand, trees, leaves, human body parts, animals, water, urine and other things are used for this protection.

Among the Yoruba there is a belief that every person has a least one enemy (known or unknown) called *ota*. There are two types of Yoruba enemies: 1) *orogun*, brought by quarrels such as land disputes, inheritance, chieftaincy titles or rivalries among wives in polygamous homes; and 2) *aye*, sorcerers, witches and all inherently wicked and malicious persons who are more dreadful than the first group. These may go to the extent of employing professional medicine persons to deal with their enemies. Potent powerful words (incantations) pronounced on charms can produce abnormal behavior, sudden loss of children or property, chronic illness and even death (Ademiluka, p. 88). There are three major ways of dealing with enemies. They are: 1) potent words (*ogede*), 2) medicine (*tira*), and 3) medicine for the body. This is an example of potent words used among Yoruba at the approach of an enemy:

O di oluworo-ji-woro	It becomes *oluworo ji-woro*
Odi oluworo-ji-woro	It becomes *oluworo ji-woro*
Oku aja kiigbo	The dead dog does not bark
Oku agbo kiikan	The dead ram does not fight
Irawe t' osubu lu odo o di'egbe	The dried leaf that falls into the river is lost forever
Od'olu woro-ji-woro	It becomes *oluworo ji-woro*
Ki awon ota mi lo gbere	So let my enemies be lost forever
Oku aja niwon	They are dead dogs
Oku agbo niwon	They are dead rams
Ewe gbigbe niwon	They are dried leaves (Agoro)

More examples of potent words for protection against witches and wizards who are considered arch-enemies of society in the African tradition are numerous; however, it suffices to mention one more. These words when recited many times would make the witches trying to attack get lost in the bush or in the cities. It will make them forget all the evil actions planned against a person reciting these potent words:

Igbagbe se oro ko lewe (3 times)	Due to forgetfulness the *oro* (cactus plant) has no leaves (3 times)
Igbagbe se afomo ka legbo (3 times)	Due to forgetfulness the *afoo* (mistletoe plant) has no roots (3 times)
Igbagbe se Olodumare ko ranti la Ese pepeye (3 times)	Due to forgetfulness, god did not remember to separate the toes of the duck (3 times)
Nijo ti pepeye ba daran egba igbe Hoho ni imu bo 'nu	When the duck is beaten it cries, *hoho*
Ki igbagbe se lagbaja omo lagbaja Ko maa wogbo lo	May forgetfulness come upon (name the enemy) the daughter of mother (that is: may he loose his senses that he or she may enter into bush
Tori t'odo ban san ki iwo ehin moo	Because a flowing river does not flow backward (Ademiluka, 71–72)

Another major way of obtaining protection against enemies is the use of charms or amulets (*tira*). These are usually obtained from medicine men, who are healers and diviners. They are mainly used to prevent witches, wizards and evil spirits from entering a house to attack a person or to nullify all attempts at evil perpetrated by enemies or sorcerers. The charm or amulet is prepared from differing ingredients for specific purposes. For example, a charm to be placed on the doorframe for protection may be made of 7 leaves of certain plants and seven seeds of alligator peppers. Charms to be tied around one's neck may require alligator peppers, white and red cola-nuts and the blood of a cock. Some charms are wrapped with animal skin and sewn while others are wrapped inside pieces of cloth or paper and tied with black and white threads. Some require the exact recitation of powerful words or prayers according to the prescription of the medicine man to be effective.

When Christian missionaries arrived in Africa the converts were forbidden to use African indigenous medicine for protection. They were told potent words, talismans, and even herbal medicine were abominable to Christianity. The missionaries with good intentions to promote the kingdom of Christ built not only schools, but maternities, dispensaries and hospitals where western medicine was used. Yet, those African Christians who had access to western medicine and were able to pay for it still had difficulty dealing with the sources of the diseases and misfortunes, which they believed were witches, wizards and enemies. Missionary medicine could not deal effectively with this aspect of African belief for which they sought protection. Having thrown away their potent words, charms and traditional medicine, African Christians believed the missionaries held the source of White-man's power in the White-man's book, the Bible. Disappointed in missionary medicine, they took the Christian book into their own hands and adapting it to their own worldview on the origins of evil, searched the book in their own way. Both by excommunication and breaking away from the mission churches the AIC incorporated biblical insight into African tradition. This separation allowed Africans to search the Bible for the supposedly hidden power. The book of Psalms became the favorite book containing the power for protection and defense against enemies. Approaching the Psalms with the same method that they had used with their indigenous medicine to ward off witches and wizards they turned mostly to the imprecatory psalms as potent words, charms and medicine to combat evil forces. Although this practice has spread all over African churches, including the mainline missionary churches, AIC became the champions of this practice. For AIC members the Psalms are believed to be more powerful than the potent words of African tradition as can be seen in the lyrics of popular songs among early AIC adherents:

Ayanga si Oloogun (2x)	Away with the medicine man (Ifa Priest) (2x)
T'owo mi bate Psaamu	When I lay my hand on Psalms
Ayanga si Oloogun	Away with the medicine man (Ogunkunle, 217)

    I challenge the juju men, once I lay hold on my Psalms
    Praying with Psalm is a staff of victory
    Praying with Psalm is a great protection
    Praying with Psalm is a staff of provision
    Praying with Psalm is a virtue of healing
    Praying with Psalm is a staff of peace
    (Ositelu, 5)

While western interpretation seems to be abstract and appears to have no context, Africentric interpretation is carried out within African culture. It is only in the contextual situation that "a meaning" and 'a value" in the way the Bible is read provides African research and hermeneutics. So, Clement Ekundayo testifies to the use of Psalm 29 for protection. He says that one should use this psalm to lift up the glory of God. According to him when one reads this psalm regularly one's enemies will begin to fear the power in praise of Yahweh. "Use this psalm to magnify the Lord. Read it always and your enemies will be frightened by the power in praises and thanksgiving" (Ekundayo, *Use*, 12). According to another author, Psalm 29 is to be read seven times in order to lift up the name of God (Anonymous, ii).

As powerful words the psalms are used in medical healing. In AIC the following psalms are classified as specifically therapeutic: 1, 2, 3, 6, 16, 20, 21, 27, 28, 29, 51, 100, 102, 109, 126, and 127 (Adamo, *Exploration*, 24–27). Specific psalms are used for specific diseases; for example, Psalm 21 is used for chronic diseases, while Psalms 100, 102 and 109 are for epilepsy and Psalm 127 for fearfulness. Psalms 16, 27, 28, and 29 are for delayed pregnancy. While Psalm 29 is specifically a psalm of praise, a hymn celebrating the glory of the Lord's awesome power in the thunderstorm, African Christians recognize the power of praise also prescribed this psalm for a delayed or overdue pregnancy. Among the Yoruba Psalm 29 is called *oogun gbogbo nse*, that is, a medicine that heals all kinds of ailment. As it is understood in Africa if you continue to shower praises on the king, *oba, obi*, and the divinities such as Ogun and Oya, there is hardly anything they could not do for the praise singer. The praise arouses them to demonstrate their power, their mightiness and awesomeness. So it is for Psalm 29, this is one of the psalms used in hope for miracles and the impossible to happen.

A person who is using Psalm 29 for a specific ailment should follow specific instructions. For example, a woman with a history of overdue pregnancy does not need to go through a painful surgery, but should read this psalm twice daily accompanied with prayer in the name of *El-Ishaddi, Jehovah Shallom* (Bolarinwa, 7). A woman with a history of infant mortality should read this psalm immediately upon becoming aware of her pregnancy until the baby is born. Psalm 29 could also be read into water daily for drinking and bathing until the birth. When the baby is born the water should be used to wash the baby until it is grown; this will make the early death of the baby impossible. The psalm can also be written in four pure parchments and be kept at the four corners of the house whenever the pregnancy occurs. The mention of the name *Jehovah Shallom* is informed by the African belief, like that of ancient Hebrews, of the power in names. Knowing and mentioning the name of a person means knowing and mentioning the person's essence.

Psalm 29 is also used as a success psalm. In discussing the psalm as a success psalm it is important first of all to understand what "success" means in African tradition. In African life success is an important aspect of life and is taken very seriously. A person who passes his or her examination is said to be successful. A person who is able to marry a good wife is successful. A person whose business is doing well is also said to be successful. One who wins a case in court is a success.. Victory over a bad habit is success. Likewise, failure in school examination, failure to win a case in court, lack of favor in one's journey are all lack of success, as are failure to find a wife, divorce, dropping out of school, and unemployment. Those lacking success in African tradition go to the priest for help. One lacking success in an examination will be given a medicine called *isoye* which literally means "activator," to activate his or her memory. There is a firm assurance that the client will be successful in any examination taken if only the proper method and *isoye* is taken; an example: A combination of honey, eeran leaves, awerepe leaves and one alligator pepper (all should be burnt together and mixed with honey. The client licks from the concoction and spits it into his left palm).

Some potent words could be prescribed for success. There is a method for good sale or riches, including these potent words to be chanted very early in the morning before going out for business:

Agbe ti o no oro, ki rahun oro	*Agbe* bird who owns dye does not complaint lack of dye
Aluko ti o ni osun, ki I rahun osun	Aluko bird that owns *osun* does not complaint the lack of *osun*
Ori agbe nig be agbe de igbo aro	The destiny of *agbee* leads *agbe* to the place of dye
Arira ma je ki nrahun owo	Arira do not let me complain of lack of money
Arira ma jeki nrahun ola	Arira do not let me complain of lack of riches (Agoro)

These methods of obtaining success are transferred to Christianity based on a strong belief that the word of God is powerful, even more powerful than the traditional potent words. The book of Psalms is especially recommended for success and Psalm 29 is among the efficacious success psalms (along with 4, 8, 9, 23, 24, 27, and 46). There are additional requirements for the reading of psalms of success. A person seeking success should properly prepare a circle of candles, light them, place salt near each, and then stand in the middle to recite Psalm 29 eight times calling the holy name *Alatula Ja Ajaralhliah* seventy-two times (Adegboyjo, 23).

Psalm 29 is considered a multipurpose psalm good not only for success in examinations, but also success in securing a good wife, good girl friend, success in court cases and successful business, work and general blessing. This is based on the belief that if one praises the Lord a miracle is bound to happen and the key to miracles is to attribute to God his power and majesty while asking for any need. That is exactly what the author of Psalm 29 did.

Conclusion

There is a temptation to condemn Africentric interpretation of imprecatory psalms as fetish, magical, unchristian and uncritical; however, a closer and critical examination of this Africentric interpretation of such psalms will reveal some basic facts that make it legitimate, important and Christian. The use of Psalm 29 with the names of God shows African tradition of the recognition of the power in names. African Christians, like the ancient Hebrews, revere the name of God and believe that divine names in the Bible are powerful when recited. The recitation of such names will achieve whatever is desired—"for your name's sake." Psalm 29's use for protection against enemies and evil spirits, healing and success in life is also recognition of the fundamental belief in the power of words. The traditional African belief in certain potent words is transferred to the belief in the power inherent in the words of God in the Scripture when memorized, recited, sung and read: "He sent his words and they were healed" (Ps 107:20). The fact is that the contents of this psalm resemble some potent words (incantations) in African tradition and culture. It has the power to achieve whatever and whenever it is recited against the enemies who especially are unrepentantly wicked. What makes Psalm 29 very powerful is the mention of the name and "voice of the Lord" (*qol YHWH*). This phrase occurs seven times in the short psalm and the name of the Lord (*YHWH*) is mentioned fifteen times.

From the above, the basic differences in western and African biblical scholarship are clear. Unlike the western world where the Bible is in doubt and ceases to be the Word of God, African biblical scholars refuse to study the Bible for studying's sake alone or to conduct scholarship solely to be doing scholarship. Moreover, African reading is *communal*; it is always understood within the community. It makes a difference with whom we read. African scholars cannot afford to neglect the poor or the ordinary people in biblical interpretation as western scholars have done. African scholars read the Bible in the context of *suffering* and *poverty*, but the western scholars read the Bible in the midst of affluence and material prosperity. This is the reason why Africans read the Bible as liberation theology. Finally, genuine serious African scholarship, unlike much western scholarship, is done in the context of a *faith* commitment. The miraculous is not doubted. There is a strong belief in God who can perform miracles. His word is also a means of performing such miracles because his word is powerful and sharper than a two-edged sword (Heb 4:12). When it appears there is no way out, he provides a way. I am of the opinion that African scholars should continue to read the Bible contextually whether it is accepted by western scholars or not. It is valuable to us.

Bibliography

Adamo, David T. "Decolonizing the Psalter in Africa." *BlTh* 5 (2007) 20–38.
———. *Exploration in African Biblical Studies*. Eugene, OR: Wipf & Stock, 2001.
———. *Reading and Interpreting the Bible in African Indigenous Churches*. Eugene, OR: Wipf & Stock, 2001.
Adegboyejo, T. N. *St. Michael Prayer Book*. Lagos: Seye Ade & Sons, 1988.
Ademiluka. "The Use of Psalms in African Context." MA thesis, University of Ilorin, Nigeria, 1990.
Agoro, Tola. Department of Works, Delta State University. Abraka. Interview, 12 September 1996.
Anonymous. *Lilo Orin Dafidi fun Adura Pelu Orin Dafidi at Iwe Owe*. N.p.
Bolarinwa, J. A. *Potency and Efficacy of Psalms*. Ibadan: Oluseyi Press, n.d.
Brueggemann, Walter. *The Message of the Psalms*. Minneapolis: Augsburg, 1984.
Childs, Brevard S. "Reflections in the Modern Studies of the Psalter." In *Magnalia Dei: The Mighty Acts of God: Essays in Memory of G. Ernest Wright*, edited by Frank Moore Cross and Patrick D. Miller, Jr., 377–88. Garden City, NY: Doubleday, 1976.
Craigie, Peter C. *Psalms 1–50*. WBC 19. Waco, TX: Word, 1983.
Crenshaw, James L. *The Psalms: An Introduction*. Grand Rapids: Eerdmans, 2001.
Dietrich, Walter, and Ulrich Luz, editors. *The Bible in a World Context: An Experiment in the Contextual Hermeneutics*. Translated by Gloria Kinsler et al. Grand Rapids: Eerdmans, 2002.
Durham, John I. "Psalms." In *The Broadman Bible Commentary*, vol. 4, edited by C. J. Allen et al., 153–464. Nashville: Broadman, 1971.

Ekundayo, Clement. *Use of Psalms for Success, Mercy, and Favour of God with Special Prayer.* Ibadan: Intercel Christian Publications, 2003.

Holter, Knut. *Interpreting the Old Testament in Africa.* New York: Lang, 2006.

Ishola, S. Ademola, and Daji Aiyegboyin. *African Indigenous Churches: An Historical Perspective.* Lagos: Greater Heights, 1997.

Ogunkunle, Caleb Oladokum. "Imprecatory Psalms: Their Forms and Uses in Ancient Israel and Some Selected Churches in Nigeria." PhD dissertation, University of Ibadan, 2000.

Omoyajowo, J. A. "The Aladura Churches in Nigeria since Independence." In *Christianity in Independent Africa*, edited by E. Fashole-Luke et al., 96–110. Bloomington: Indiana University Press, 1978.

Ositelu, J. O. *The Secret of Meditation with God and the Uses of Psalms.* Ogere, Shagamu: Publication Department, Church of the Lord Aladura Worldwide, n.d.

Ukpong, Justin. "Inculturation Hermeneutics: An African Approach to Biblical Interpretation." In *The Bible in a World Context: An Experiment in the Contextual Hermeneutics*, edited by Walter Dietrich and Ulrich Luz, 17–32. Translated by Gloria Kinsler et al. Grand Rapids: Eerdmans, 2002.

West, Gerald O. *The Academy of the Poor: Towards a Dialogical Reading of the Bible.* Sheffield: Sheffield Academic, 1999.

Index of Proper Names

Abraham	29, 43–46	Brock, Sebastian	56
Abraham ben Ezra	72	Bruegemann, Walter	134
Adam	32	Bruno of Segni	73–75
Adejobi, Adeleke	129		
Akinswon, Abiodun	128	Calvin, John	79, 84–89, 95, 102, 105–6, 110
Alexander the Great	55		
Alexander, William	85	Cassian	73–74
Ambrose of Milan	26–27, 32–33, 94	Cassiodorus	90
		Chamberlain, Gary	112
Andrew of St. Victor	70	Childs, Brevard	134
Anselm of Canterbury	73	Chromatius	26–27, 33
Aquila	60	Cowe, S. Peter	59
Arnobius Junior	26–27	Craigie, Peter C.	90–91
Aristotle	87	Cranmer, Thomas	95
Athanasius	26, 64	Cyril	26–27
Augustine	26–27, 30, 32–35, 70, 73, 79–83		
		Dahood, Mitchell	90
		Daniel of Ṣalah	59–60, 64–65
Babalola, Joseph Ayo	127–28, 131	David	2, 30–32, 34, 37, 39–42, 44–45, 47–50, 57–59, 62, 64, 86–87, 133
Bar Daisan	56		
Basil of Caesarea	26, 28, 30–31, 62, 64, 94		
		Daw, Carl	107
Bede, The Venerable	26	Day, John	123–24
Bell, John	107	De Beze, Theodore	95
Bellarmin, Robert	4	Didymus Caecus	26–27
Berthier, Jacques	112	Diodorus of Tarsus	26, 28–29, 32–33, 57
Booth, William	126		
Braude, William G.	45	Dionysius Bar Salibi	59, 62–64

Ekundayo, Clement	138	Kimchi, David	70–73
Elijah	69	Kloos, Carola	90–91
Ephraem the Syrian	26–27, 56	Korah	76
Epiphanius	64		
Eusebius	26	Loco, David Hodonu	129
Ezra	48	Luther, Martin	11, 20–23, 79–86, 88–89, 102, 105, 110
Freedman, David Noel	90		
		Marot, Clement	85, 95
Gamaliel II	49	Maximus of Turin	26–27
Gregory Bar Hebraeus	59, 62, 64–66	Moses	29, 40–42, 45, 60, 71, 76, 92
Gregory of Nyssa	26–27, 31	Moshe Bar Kepha	59, 61–62
Gregory the Great	26, 73	Mowinkel, Sigmund	91, 133
Gunkel, Hermann	91, 133	Muilenburg, James	134
		Münster, Sebastian	85
Haugen, Marty	111		
Hezekiah	28–29, 57–58, 61, 64–65, 91	Nebuchadnezzar	43
		Nicholas of Lyra	70, 76–77
Hippolytus	26–27, 31, 64	Noah	19–20, 31, 35
Hopkins, John	107		
Hosea	116–17, 124	Odubanjo, Pastor	128
Hugh of St. Cher	75–76	Oduwole, Apostle	129
Hugh of St. Victor	70	Oecumenius	26
Hyland, C. Franke	90	O'Keefe, John J.	60
		Olayemi, Elder	128
Isaac	43–46, 49	Oluwalowo, Josiah	128–29, 131
Ishodad of Merv	59–61	Origen	26–27, 64, 70
		Orimolade, Moses	131
Jacob	43, 45–46, 49	Oshitelu	see Oluwalowo, Josiah
James VI of Scotland and I of England	85	Oshoffa, Samuel Bilewu Joseph	129–31
Jerome	14–19, 26–27, 77, 79, 81, 83	Paul (Apostle)	70, 81
Jesus (Christ)	3, 29–35, 62, 65, 69, 73–76, 80–84, 94–95, 97, 104–5, 107	Perry, Michael	109
		Peter (Apostle)	74
		Peter Chrysologus	26–27
John (Apostle)	74	Peter Lombard	74–75
John Chrysostom	26–27, 94	Phineas	49
John of Damascus	26	Pius X, Pope	95
John the Baptist	31, 74, 94	Procopius	26
Johnson, Ben	25		
Joseph (father of Jesus)	32	Rashi	see Solomon ben Isaac
Josiah	91	Rashbam	see Samuel ben Meir

Rufinus	26–27
Ryan, Stephen D.	63
Samuel ben Meir [Rashbam]	70–72
Schaeffer, Claude	118
Schoening, Dale A.	109
Seerveld, Calvin	108
Sennacherib	32–33
Severianus	26
Shield, Prophet	129
Smith, Geoffrey Boulton	112
Solomon	60
Solomon ben Isaac [Rashi]	70–72, 92
Somoye, Prophet	129
Sophronius	94
Sternhold, Thomas	107
Swain, Larry	25
Symmachus	60
Theodore of Mopsuestia	26, 28–29, 32–33, 57–58, 60–61, 64–65
Theodoret of Cyrus	4, 26–29, 33
Theodotian	60
Tunolase, Moses Orimolade	128
Venter, Peter M.	90
Vosté, J. M.	62
Warner, Steven	112
Warren, Norman	109
Watts, Isaac	107–8, 113
Weimer, Chris	25
Weiser, Arthur	91
Wesley, Charles	5–6, 112

www.ingramcontent.com/pod-product-compliance
Lightning Source LLC
Chambersburg PA
CBHW070908160426
43193CB00011B/1404